W9-BJV-498

THE AMERICAN PRESIDENCY

CLINTON ROSSITER

The American Presidency

HARCOURT, BRACE AND COMPANY
NEW YORK

LIBRARY OF CONGRESS CATALOG CARD NUMBER: 56-6660

PRINTED IN THE UNITED STATES OF AMERICA

To My Students, Past and Present, in
Government 216
Cornell University

"Methought I heard a voice cry, 'Sleep no more!' "
—*Macbeth*, II, i, 36

This book is a revised version of six lectures given on the Charles R. Walgreen Foundation at the University of Chicago, April 23-May 3, 1956. I am grateful to the officers of the Foundation for giving me this opportunity to rethink the thoughts of fifteen years on the Presidency. I am also grateful to James M. Burns, Edward S. Corwin, Arch Dotson, Richard P. Longaker, Alexander J. Morin, Richard E. Neustadt, J. Francis Paschal, John P. Roche, and, most of all, Mary Crane Rossiter, for their help and advice.

CLINTON ROSSITER

Ithaca, New York
March, 1956

CONTENTS

THE AMERICAN PRESIDENCY

CHAPTER 1

THE POWERS OF THE PRESIDENCY

★

Sometimes the stranger outside the gates has a clearer vision of an American institution than we who have lived with it all our lives. John Bright, best friend in all England of the embattled Union, paid this tribute to the Presidency in 1861:

> We know what an election is in the United States for President of the Republic. . . . Every four years there springs from the vote created by the whole people a President over that great nation. I think the whole world offers no finer spectacle than this; it offers no higher dignity; and there is no greater object of ambition on the political stage on which men are permitted to move. You may point, if you will, to hereditary rulers, to crowns coming down through successive generations of the same family, to thrones based on prescription or on conquest, to sceptres wielded over veteran legions and subject realms,—but to my mind there is nothing more worthy of reverence and obedience, and nothing more sacred, than the authority of the freely chosen magistrate of a great and free people; and if there be on earth and amongst men any right divine to govern, surely it rests with a ruler so chosen and so appointed.

My purpose is to make good Bright's splendid judgment by examining coolly at a hot time the powers and limits, the strengths and weaknesses, the past and present and future of the American Presidency. This book is very far from a detailed or definitive portrait of the office. It is at best an impressionistic rendering of the main dimensions, and I beg early forgiveness for all the things I cannot possibly find room to say about it. My hope is simply that those who read these chapters may come to a sharper understanding

position the Presidency occupies in the annals of
st and the hopes of our future.

is cool examination must begin with a careful accounting of those tasks the President performs in our system of
government, for if there is any one thing about our highest
office that strikes the eye immediately, it is the staggering
number of duties we have laid upon its incumbent. Those
who cherish Gilbert and Sullivan will remember Pooh-Bah,
the "particularly haughty and exclusive person" in *The
Mikado,* who filled the offices of "First Lord of the Treasury,
Lord Chief Justice, Commander-in-Chief, Lord High Admiral, Master of the Buckhounds, Groom of the Back Stairs,
Archbishop of Titipu, and Lord Mayor, both acting and
elect." We chuckle at the fictitious Pooh-Bah; we can only
wonder at the real one that history has made of the American President. He has at least three jobs for every one of
Pooh-Bah's, and they are not performed with the flick of a
lacquered fan. At the risk of being perhaps too analytical,
let me review the functions of the modern President. These,
as I interpret them, are the major roles he plays in the
sprawling drama of American government:

First, the President is Chief of State. He remains today,
as he has always been, the ceremonial head of the government of the United States, and he must take part with real
or apparent enthusiasm in a range of activities that would
keep him running and posing from sunrise to bedtime if
he were not protected by a cold-blooded staff. Some of these
activities are solemn or even priestly in nature; others,
through no fault of his own, are flirtations with vulgarity.
The long catalogue of public duties that the Queen discharges in England, the President of the Republic in France,
and the Governor-General in Canada is the President's responsibility in this country, and the catalogue is even longer
because he is not a king, or even the agent of one, and is
therefore expected to go through some rather undignified
paces by a people who think of him as a combination of
scoutmaster, Delphic oracle, hero of the silver screen, and
father of the multitudes.

As figurehead rather than working head of our government, he greets distinguished visitors from all parts of the world, lays wreaths on the tomb of the Unknown Soldier and before the statue of Lincoln, makes proclamations of thanksgiving and commemoration, bestows the Medal of Honor on flustered pilots, holds state dinners for the diplomatic corps and the Supreme Court, lights the nation's Christmas tree, buys the first poppy from the Veterans of Foreign Wars, gives the first crisp banknote to the Red Cross, throws out the first ball for the Senators (the nine, not the ninety-six), rolls the first egg for the Easter Bunny, and in the course of any month greets a fantastic procession of firemen, athletes, veterans, Boy Scouts, Campfire Girls, boosters, hog callers, exchange students, and heroic school children. The March of Dimes or the Community Chest Drive could not possibly get under way without a five-minute telecast from the White House; Sunday isn't Sunday if the President and his lady skip church; a public works project isn't public until the President presses a silver key in Washington and explodes a charge of dynamite in Fort Peck or Hanford or the Tennessee Valley.

The President is not permitted to confine this sort of activity to the White House and the city around it. The people expect him to come to them from time to time, and the presidential grand tour, a precedent set conspicuously by George Washington, is an important aspect of the ceremonial function. Nor is this function, for obvious political and cultural reasons, untainted with commercialism. If it isn't one "Week" for him to proclaim or salute it's another, and what President, especially in an election year, would turn away the Maid of Cotton or the Railroad Man of the Year, or, to keep everybody happy, the Truck Driver of the Year from the White House door?

The President, in short, is the one-man distillation of the American people just as surely as the Queen is of the British people; he is, in President Taft's words, "the personal embodiment and representative of their dignity and majesty." (Mr. Taft, it will be remembered, was uniquely shaped by nature's lavish hand to be a personal embodiment of dignity and majesty.) The role of Chief of State may often seem trivial, yet it cannot be neglected by a President who proposes to stay in favor and, more to the point, in touch with the people, the ultimate source of all his power. It is a conspicuous thief of his precious time, yet more than one President has played it in such a way as to gain genuine release from the routine tasks and hard decisions that fill the rest of his day.

And whether or not he enjoys this role, no President can fail to realize that all his powers are invigorated, indeed are given a new dimension of authority, because he is the symbol of our sovereignty, continuity, and grandeur. When he asks a Senator to lunch in order to enlist his support for a pet project, when he thumps his desk and reminds the antagonists in a labor dispute of the larger interests of the American people, when he orders a general to cease caviling or else be removed from his command, the Senator and the disputants and the general are well aware—especially if the scene is laid in the White House—that they are dealing with no ordinary head of government. The framers of the Constitution took a momentous step when they fused the dignity of a king and the power of a prime minister in one elective office.

The second of the President's roles is that of Chief Executive. He reigns, but he also rules; he symbolizes the people, but he also runs their government. "The true test of a good government is its aptitude and tendency to produce a good administration," Hamilton wrote in *The Federalist*, at the same time making clear that it would be the first duty of the proposed President to produce this "good administration." For reasons that I shall touch upon later, the President—and I mean any President, no matter how happily he may wallow in the details of administration—has more trouble playing this role successfully than he does any of the others. It is, in fact, the one major area of presidential activity in which his powers are simply not equal to his responsibilities. Yet the role is an important one, and we cannot savor the fullness of the President's duties unless we recall that he is held primarily and often exclusively accountable for the ethics, loyalty, efficiency, frugality, and responsiveness to the public's wishes of the two and a third million Americans in the national administration.

Both the Constitution and Congress have recognized his power to supervise the day-to-day activities of the executive branch, strained and restrained though it may often be in practice. From the Constitution, explicitly or implicitly, he receives the twin powers of appointment and removal, as well as the primary duty, which no law or plan or circumstance can ever take away from him, to "take care that the laws be faithfully executed." He alone may appoint, with the advice and consent of the Senate, the several thousand top officials who run the government; he alone may remove, with varying degrees of abruptness, those who are not executing the laws faithfully. The power of removal—the "gun behind the door"—is the symbol and final sanction of his position as Chief Executive. I doubt that there has ever been a more dramatic vindication of the President's authority "to produce a good administration" than Mr. Roosevelt's cashiering of Dr. A. E. Morgan from the chairmanship of the Tennessee Valley Authority in 1938. Frustrated in his attempts to secure Dr. Morgan's co-operation in clearing up a nasty clash of personalities that had brought the activities of T.V.A.'s governing board to a standstill, the President removed him peremptorily, made a new appointment to the position, and sent T.V.A. about its business. There were screams of anguish and prophecies of dictatorship, but there was no effective challenge to the President's contention that, although he could not construe Morgan's duties for him nor substitute his own judgment for that of a board rendered independent by statute, he could and must act to keep T.V.A. in operation.

From Congress, through such legislative mandates as the Budget and Accounting Act of 1921 and the succession of Reorganization Acts, the President has received further acknowledgment of his administrative leadership. Although independent agencies such as the Interstate Commerce Commission and the National Labor Relations Board operate by design outside his immediate area of responsibility, most of the government's administrative tasks are still carried on within the fuzzy-edged pyramid that has the President at its lonely peak; the laws that are executed daily in his name and under his general supervision are numbered in the hundreds. One task illustrates the scope of the President's administrative responsibility: the preparation and execution of the federal budget. One program attests the power he wields over the public's servants: the loyalty standards instituted by President Truman's Executive Order 9835 of March 21, 1947 and tightened by President Eisenhower's Executive Order 10450 of April 29, 1953. One passage from the *United States Code* makes clear that Congress itself expects much of him:

> The President is authorized to prescribe such regulations for the admission of persons into the civil service of the United States as may best promote the efficiency thereof, and ascertain the fitness of each candidate in respect to age, health, character, knowledge, and ability for the branch of service into which he seeks to enter; and for this purpose he may employ suitable persons to conduct such inquiries, and may prescribe their duties, and establish regulations for the conduct of persons who may receive appointment in the civil service.

It might be useful to hear the most recent opinion of the experts in this field. I take these paragraphs from the report of the sixth American Assembly, which met at Arden House in October 1954 to consider the "character, prestige, and problems" of the public service:

> *The President* has the responsibility for leadership of the Executive Branch of the Federal Government service. Constitutional principles, the necessities of our national life and the example of successful corporate enterprise all underscore the indispensability of executive responsibility for the personnel policies and the personnel management of the Federal Government.
> This leadership must be acknowledged and supported by the heads and employees of executive departments, by the party leaders and by

the members of the Congress. This leadership must be accepted and exercised by the President, if the business of the National Government is to be efficiently performed.

Whether it is his letters or his taxes that the ordinary citizen wants more efficiently collected, he looks first of all to the President as business manager of the administration. There was a time when Presidents could and did pay strict attention to matters such as these, and about a hundred million people still do not seem to realize that the time has passed.

Next, the President is Chief Diplomat. Although authority in the field of foreign relations is shared constitutionally among three organs—President, Congress, and, for two special purposes, the Senate—his position is paramount, if not indeed dominant. In 1799 John Marshall, no particular friend of executive power, spoke of the President as "the sole organ of the nation in its external relations, and its sole representative with foreign nations." In 1936 Justice Sutherland, no particular friend of executive power and even less of Franklin D. Roosevelt, put the Court's stamp of approval on "the very delicate, plenary and exclusive power of the President as the sole organ of the government in the field of international relations."

The primacy of the executive comes under vigorous attack from time to time, chiefly from those who object to a specific policy even more strongly than to a President's pursuit of it, and it is true that he acts more arbitrarily and independently than the framers of the Constitution ever intended him to act. Yet the growth of presidential authority in this area seems to have been almost inevitable, and hardly the outcome of a shameful conspiracy by the three Democratic Presidents of the twentieth century. Constitution, laws, custom, the practice of other nations, and the logic of history have combined to place the President in a dominant position. Secrecy, dispatch, unity, continuity, and access to information—the ingredients of successful diplomacy—are properties of his office, and Congress, I need hardly add, possesses none of them.

This field can be conveniently if somewhat inexactly divided into two sectors: the formulation of policy and the conduct of affairs. The first of these is a joint undertaking in which the President proposes, Congress disposes, and the wishes of the people prevail in the end. The President's leadership is usually vindicated. Our most ancient and honored policy is significantly known as the *Monroe* Doctrine; our leading policy of the past ten years has been the *Truman* Doctrine. From Washington's Proclamation of Neutrality in 1793 to Eisenhower's decision to go to the Summit in 1955, the President has repeatedly committed the nation to decisive attitudes and actions abroad, more than once to war itself. Occasionally Congress has compelled him to abandon a policy already put forward, as it did in the case of Grant's plans for Santo Domingo, or has forced distasteful policies upon him, as it did upon Madison in 1812 and McKinley in 1898. Nevertheless, a stubborn President is hard to budge, a crusading President hard to thwart. The diplomatic lives of the two Roosevelts are proof enough of these assertions. Mr. Truman was not exaggerating much when he told an informal gathering of the Jewish War Veterans in 1948: "I make American foreign policy."

The transaction of business with foreign nations is, as Jefferson once wrote, "executive altogether," and Congress finds it difficult to exercise effective control or to deliver constructive criticism—not that Congress can be accused of lack of trying. The State Department carries on its many activities in the name of the President, and he is or ought to be in command of every procedure through which our foreign relations are carried on from one day to the next: negotiation of treaties and executive agreements, recognition of new governments and nations, selection and supervision of diplomatic personnel, adjustment of tariff barriers within statutory limits, direction of our delegation to the United Nations, and communications with foreign powers. As Commander in Chief he deploys our armed forces abroad and occasionally supports our policies with what is known as "presidential warmaking." The conduct of foreign relations as a short-range proposition is a presidential prerogative, and short-range actions—the recognition of a revolutionary regime in Argentina, the reception of a Burmese prime minister, the raising of the duty on Swiss watches—can have long-range consequences.

In recent years, the role of Chief Diplomat has become the most important and exacting of all those we call on the President to play. Indeed, when one thinks of the hours of "prayerful consideration" President Eisenhower devotes each week to briefing sessions with John Foster Dulles and Dillon Anderson, conferences with the National Security Council, lunches with Senators George and Knowland, explanatory and inspirational speeches to the nation, and lonely wrestling bouts with appointments and reports and messages to Congress—not to mention his correspondence with Marshal Zhukov and Premier Bulganin—it is a wonder that he has a moment's time for any of his other duties.

The President's fourth major function is one he could not escape if he wished, and several Presidents have wished it mightily. The Constitution designates him specifically as "Commander-in-Chief of the Army and Navy of the United States, and of the militia of the several States when called into the actual service of the United States." In peace and war he is the supreme commander of the armed forces, the living guarantee of the American belief in "the supremacy of the civil over military authority."

In time of peace he raises, trains, supervises, and deploys the forces that Congress is willing to maintain. With the aid of the Secretary of Defense, the Joint Chiefs of Staff, and the National Security Council—all of whom are his personal choices—he looks constantly to the state of the nation's defenses. He is never for one day allowed to forget that he will be held accountable by people, Congress, and history for the nation's readiness to meet an enemy assault. There is no more striking indication of the present latitude of the President's military power than these matter-of-fact words in the Atomic Energy Act of 1946:

Sec. 6(a) *Authority.* The Commission is authorized to—

(1) conduct experiments and do research and development work in the military application of atomic energy; and

(2) engage in the production of atomic bombs, atomic bomb parts, or other military weapons utilizing fissionable materials; except that such activities shall be carried on only to the extent that the express consent and direction of the President of the United States has been obtained, which consent and direction shall be obtained at least once each year.

The President from time to time may direct the Commission (1) to deliver such quantities of fissionable materials or weapons to the armed forces for such use as he deems necessary in the interest of the national defense or (2) to authorize the armed forces to manufacture, produce, or acquire any equipment or device utilizing fissionable material or atomic energy as a military weapon.

It should be added that, despite the wounded protests of Senator Bricker, most citizens agreed with Mr. Truman's brisk assertion in 1950 that it was for the President to decide whether the H-bomb should be built. And, as the same man demonstrated in 1945, it is for the President to decide in time of war when and where and whether it should be dropped.

In such time, "when the blast of war blows in our ears," the President's power to command the forces swells out of all proportion to his other powers. All major decisions of strategy, and many of tactics as well, are his alone to make or to approve. Lincoln and Franklin Roosevelt, each in his own way and time, showed how far the power of military command can be driven by a President anxious to have his generals and admirals get on with the war. No small part of his time, as we know from Lincoln's experience, can be spent searching for the right generals and admirals.

But this, the power of command, is only a fraction of the vast responsibility the modern President draws from the Commander-in-Chief clause. The framers of the Constitution, to be sure, took a narrow view of the authority granted in this clause. "It would amount," Hamilton wrote offhandedly in *The Federalist*, "to nothing more than the supreme command and direction of the military and naval forces, as first General and Admiral of the Confederacy." This view of presidential power as something purely military foundered on the hard facts of the first of our modern wars. Faced by an overriding necessity for harsh, even dictatorial action, Lincoln used the Commander-in-Chief clause— at first gingerly, in the end boldly—to justify an unprecedented series of measures that cut deeply into the accepted liberties of the people and the routine pattern of government. Wilson added another cubit to the stature of the wartime Presidency by demanding that Congress give him those powers over the economy about which there was any constitutional doubt, and Franklin Roosevelt, who had read about Lincoln and lived with Wilson, carried the wartime Presidency to breath-taking heights of authority over the American economy and social order. The creation and staffing of a whole array of emergency boards and offices, the seizure and operation of more than sixty strike-bound or strike-threatened plants and industries, and the forced evacuation of 70,000 American citizens of Japanese descent from the West Coast are three massive examples of what a President can do as Commander in Chief to stiffen the home front in support of the fighting forces. It is important to recall that Congress came to Roosevelt's aid in each of these series of actions by passing laws empowering him to do what he had done already or by fixing penalties for violating the orders of his subordinates. Congress, too, likes to win wars, and Congressmen are more likely to needle the President for inactivity and timidity than to accuse him of acting too swiftly and arbitrarily.

Now that total war, which ignores the old line between battlefield and home front, has been compounded by the absolute weapon, which ignores every rule we have ever tried to honor, we may expect the President to be nothing short of a "constitutional dictator" in the event of war. The next wartime President, who may well be our last, will have the right, of which Lincoln spoke with feeling, to take "any measure which may best subdue the enemy."

The President's duties are not all purely executive in nature. He is also intimately associated, by Constitution and custom, with the legislative process, and we may therefore consider him to be the Chief Legislator. Congress still has its strong men, but the complexity of the problems it is asked to solve by a people who assume that all problems are solvable has made *external* leadership a requisite of effective operation. The President alone is in a political, constitutional, and practical position to provide such leadership, and he is therefore expected, within the limits of constitutional and political propriety, to guide Congress in much of its lawmaking activity. Indeed, since Congress is no longer minded or organized to guide itself, the refusal or inability of the President to serve as leader results in weak and disorganized government.

Success in the delicate area of executive-legislative relations depends on several variables: the political complexion of President and Congress, the state of the Union and of the world around us, the vigor and tact of the President's leadership, and the mood of Congress, which is generally friendly near the beginning of a President's term and rebellious near the end. Yet even the President whose announced policy is to "restore our hallowed system of the separation of powers" and leave Congress strictly alone—Coolidge is a capital example, one not likely to be repeated—must exercise his constitutional option to veto or not to veto about a thousand times each session, must discourse once a year on the state of the Union and occasionally recommend "such measures as he shall judge necessary and expedient," must present the annual budget, and must make some effort to realize at least the less controversial promises in his party's platform. In the hands of a Wilson or a Roosevelt, and now in the hands of an Eisenhower, the Presidency becomes a sort of prime ministership or "third House of

Congress," and the chief concern of the President is to push for the enactment of his own or his party's legislative desires.

Upon many of our most celebrated laws the presidential imprint is clearly stamped. Each of these was drafted in the President's offices, introduced and supported by his friends, defended in committee by his aides, voted through by a party over which every form of discipline and persuasion was exerted, and then made law by his signature. The signature, of course, was affixed with several dozen fountain pens, which were then passed out among the beaming friends and aides. Among the "ploys and gambits" the President may have used in the process were the White House breakfast with his chief lieutenants, or perhaps with his chief obstructionists; the fireside chat with his constituents, some of whom were also constituents of the obstructionists; the press conference, in which he proclaimed his astonishment at the way Congress was dragging its feet; the dangled patronage or favor, which brought a wavering or even hostile Senator to his side; and the threat of a veto, which he brandished like the Gorgon's head to frighten the mavericks into removing objectionable amendments to the bill he had first sent over.

Even the President who lacks a congressional majority must go through the motions of leadership; and if, like President Eisenhower, his majority position in the country overmatches his minority position in Congress, he will be expected by the country, and therefore by Congress, to turn his policies into law. The Republicans always waited politely for Mr. Truman's proposals on labor, taxes, inflation, civil rights, and education, however scant the regard they intended to pay them. The Democrats, if we may believe Speaker Rayburn and Senator Johnson, have been impatient to hear President Eisenhower's proposals and to feel the lash of his leadership. In any case, the chief responsibility for bridging the constitutional gulf between executive and legislature now rests irrevocably with the President. His tasks as leader of Congress are difficult and delicate, yet he must bend to them steadily or be judged a failure. The President

who will not give his best thoughts to guiding Congress, more
so the President who is temperamentally or politically un-
fitted to "get along with Congress," is now rightly considered
a national liability.

Chief of State, Chief Executive, Chief Diplomat, Commander
in Chief, Chief Legislator—these functions make up the
strictly constitutional burden of the President. As Mr.
Truman himself allowed in several of his folksy sermons
on the Presidency, they form an aggregate of power that
would have made Caesar or Genghis Khan or Napoleon bite
his nails with envy. Yet even these do not fill out the whole
range of presidential responsibility. I count at least five additional limbs that have been grafted onto the original trunk.

The first of these is the President's role as Chief of Party,
one that he has played by popular demand and to a mixed
reception ever since the administration of Thomas Jefferson.
However sincere Washington's abhorrence of "factions" may
have been, his own administration and policies spawned our
first two parties, and their arrival upon the scene altered
the character of the Presidency radically. No matter how
fondly or how often we may long for a President who is
above the heat of party strife, we must acknowledge resolutely his right and duty to be the leader of his party. He is
at once the least political and most political of all heads
of government.

The value of this function has been attested by all our
first-rate Presidents. Jackson, Lincoln, Wilson, and the
two Roosevelts were especially skillful party leaders. By
playing the politician with unashamed zest the first of these
gave his epic administration a unique sense of cohesion, the
second rallied doubting Republican leaders and their fol-
lowings to the cause of the Union, and the other three
achieved genuine triumphs as catalysts of congressional action. That gifted amateur, Dwight D. Eisenhower, has also
played the role for every drop of drama and power in it. It
would have astonished George Washington, but it cannot
even ruffle us, to learn that the President devoted breakfast

and most of the morning of June 20, 1955—a day otherwise given over to solemn celebration of the tenth birthday of the United Nations—to mending a few fences with Republican leaders of California. He was demonstrating only what close observers of the Presidency know well: that its incumbent must devote an hour or two of every working day to the profession of Chief Democrat or Chief Republican. The President dictates the selection of the national chairman and other top party officials, reminds his partisans in Congress that the legislative record must be bright if victory is to crown their joint efforts, delivers "fight talks" to the endless procession of professionals who call upon him, and, through the careful distribution of the loaves and fishes of federal patronage, keeps the party a going concern. The loaves and fishes are not so plentiful as they were in the days of Jackson and Lincoln, but he is still a wholesale distributor of "jobs for the boys."

It troubles many good people, not entirely without reason, to watch their dignified Chief of State dabbling in politics, smiling on party hacks, and endorsing candidates he knows to be unfit for anything but immediate delivery to the county jail. Yet if he is to persuade Congress, if he is to achieve a loyal and cohesive administration, if he is to be elected in the first place (and re-elected in the second), he must put his hand firmly to the plow of politics. The working head of government in a constitutional democracy must be the nation's number-one boss, and most Presidents have had no trouble swallowing this truth.

Yet he is, at the same time if not in the same breath, the Voice of the People, the leading formulator and expounder of public opinion in the United States. While he acts as political leader of some, he serves as moral spokesman for all. Well before Woodrow Wilson had come to the Presidency, but not before he had begun to dream of it, he expressed the essence of this role:

His is the only national voice in affairs. Let him once win the admiration and confidence of the country, and no other single force can withstand him, no combination of forces will easily overpower him.

His position takes the imagination of the country. He is the representative of no constituency, but of the whole people. When he speaks
in his true character, he speaks for no special interest. If he rightly
interpret the national thought and boldly insist upon it, he is irresistible; and the country never feels the zest for action so much as
when its President is of such insight and calibre.

Throughout our history there have been moments of
triumph or dedication or frustration or even shame when the
will of the people—the General Will, I suppose we could
call it—demanded to be heard clearly and unmistakably. It
took the line of Presidents some time to grasp the meaning
of this function, but since the day when Andrew Jackson
thundered against the Nullifiers of South Carolina no effective President has doubted his prerogative to speak the
people's mind on the great issues of his time, to act, again
in Wilson's words, as "the spokesman for the real sentiment and purpose of the country." The coming of the radio,
and now of television, has added immeasurably to the range
and power of his voice. Neither Jackie Gleason nor Ed
Sullivan, neither George Gobel nor Edward R. Murrow—
not even, I would insist, the peddlers of Revlon lipstick—
can gain access to so many millions of American homes. Indeed, the President must be especially on his guard not
to pervert these might channels and debase representative
government. It is one thing for a huckster to appeal to the
people to buy a mouthwash, quite another for a President
to appeal to them to stampede the Senate.

Sometimes, of course, it is no easy thing, even for the
most sensitive and large-minded of Presidents, to know
the real sentiment of the people or to be bold enough to
state it in defiance of loudly voiced contrary opinion. Yet the
President who senses the popular mood and spots new tides
even before they start to run, who practices shrewd economy
in his appearances as spokesman for the nation, who is
conscious of his unique power to compel discussion on his
own terms, and who talks the language of Christian morality and the American tradition, can shout down any other
voice or chorus of voices in the land. There have been

times, to be sure, when we seemed as willing to listen to an antagonist as to the President—to Senator Taft in 1950, General MacArthur in 1951, Clarence Randall of Inland Steel in June 1952—but in the end, we knew, and the antagonist knew, too, that the battle was no Armageddon, that it was being fought between grossly ill-matched forces.

The President is the American people's one authentic trumpet, and he has no higher duty than to give a clear and certain sound. "Words at great moments of history are deeds," Clement Attlee said of Winston Churchill on the day the latter stepped down in 1945. The strong and imaginative President can make with his own words the kind of history that Churchill made in 1940 and 1941. When the events of 1933 are all but forgotten, we shall still recall Roosevelt's words, "The only thing we have to fear is fear itself."

In the memorable case of *In re Neagle* (1890), which still makes good reading for those who like a touch of horse opera in their constitutional law, Justice Samuel Miller spoke with feeling of the "peace of the United States"—a happy condition, it would appear, of domestic tranquillity and national prosperity that is often broken by violent men and forces and just as often restored by the President. Perhaps the least known of his functions is the mandate he holds—from the Constitution and the laws, but even more positively from the people of the United States—to act as Protector of the Peace. The emergencies that can disturb the peace of the United States seem to grow thicker and more vexing every year, and hardly a week now goes by that the President is not called upon to take forceful steps in behalf of a section or city or group or enterprise that has been hit hard and suddenly by disaster. Generally, it is for state and local authorities to deal with social and natural calamities, but in the face of a riot in Detroit or floods in New England or a railroad strike in Chicago or a panic in Wall Street the people turn almost instinctively to the White House and its occupant for aid and comfort.

And he, certainly, is the person to give it. No man or combination of men in the United States can muster up so quickly and authoritatively the troops, experts, food, money, loans, equipment, medical supplies, and moral support that may be needed in a disaster. Are thousands of homes flooded in the Missouri and Ohio Valleys?—then the President will order Coast Guardsmen and their boats to be flown to the scene for rescue and patrol work, and he will go himself to bring cheer to the homeless. Are cattle starving on the snow-bound western plains?—then the President will order the Air Force to engage in Operation Haylift. Are the farmers of Rhode Island and Massachusetts facing ruin in the wake of a September hurricane?—then the President will designate these states as disaster areas and order the Secretary of Agriculture to release surplus foods and make emergency loans on easy terms. Or are we having a March 1933 all over again, and are we caught up in the first dreadful moments of a financial panic?—then the President will issue the necessary orders on the authority of two laws that have been waiting quietly on the books since the first year of the New Deal:

Section 4 of the Emergency Banking Act of 1933:

In order to provide for the safer and more effective operation of the National Banking System . . . during such emergency period as the President of the United States by proclamation may prescribe, no member bank of the Federal Reserve System shall transact any banking business except to such extent and subject to such regulations, limitations and restrictions as may be prescribed by the Secretary of the Treasury, with the approval of the President.

Section 19 (a) of the Securities Exchange Act of 1934:

The Commission is authorized . . . if in its opinion the public interest so requires, summarily to suspend trading in any registered security on any national securities exchange for a period not exceeding ten days, or with the approval of the President, summarily to suspend all trading on any national securities exchange for a period not exceeding ninety days.

In short, the President has been statutorily empowered in the event of any future panic like that of March 1933 to declare what amounts to financial martial law. At the same time, he remains constitutionally, even extra-constitutionally empowered in the event of an atomic attack to declare straight-out martial law through all the land. This, it will be remembered, is exactly what President Eisenhower pretended to do in the simulated hydrogen bomb attack of June 1955. One of the remarkable events of that three-day test of our readiness for atomic war was the startled discovery by Mr. Eisenhower and his staff that "the inherent powers of the Presidency," something about which Republicans usually maintain uneasy silence, would be the nation's chief crutch in the aftermath of the ultimate disaster. This fact, and thus his status as Protector of the Peace, had already been recognized by a group of Senators who called on Mr. Eisenhower to "assume personal responsibility" for creating an adequate program of civil defense.

In one area of American life, the economy in whose health most of the world now has a stake, the people of this country are no longer content to let disaster fall upon them unopposed. They now expect their government, and especially their President, to prevent a depression or panic and not simply to wait until one has developed before putting it to rout. Thus the President has a new function, which is still taking shape, that of Manager of Prosperity.

The origin of this function can be fixed with unusual exactness. The Employment Act of 1946 was the first clear acknowledgment by the federal government of a general responsibility for maintaining a stable and prosperous economy:

Sec. 2. The Congress hereby declares that it is the continuing policy and responsibility of the Federal Government to use all practicable means consistent with its needs and obligations and other essential considerations of national policy, with the assistance and cooperation of industry, agriculture, labor, and State and local governments, to coordinate and utilize all its plans, functions, and resources for the purpose of creating and maintaining, in a manner calculated to foster and promote free competitive enterprise and the general welfare, conditions under which there will be afforded useful employment opportunities, including self-employment, for those able, willing, and seeking to work, and to promote maximum employment, production, and purchasing power.

The significant feature of this law from our point of view is the deliberate manner in which, in section after section, the President is singled out as the official who is "to foster and promote free competitive enterprise, to avoid economic fluctuations or to diminish the effects thereof, and to maintain employment, production, and purchasing power." He is granted the splendid gift of the Council of Economic Advisers; he is requested to make the annual Economic Report and such supplementary reports as may be advisable; he is expected to propose "a program for carrying out the policy declared in section 2, together with such recommendations for legislation as he may deem necessary or desirable." There is apparently no doubt in Congress's collective mind that one of the President's prime duties is to watch like a mother hen over all the eggs in all our baskets. As for the American people, it is a notorious fact that we give our President small credit for prosperity and full blame for hard times.

Yet even if the Employment Act had never been passed, he would have this duty and most of the powers that go with it. We have built some remarkable stabilizing devices into our political economy since 1929, and the men who control them—in the Federal Reserve System, the Securities and Exchange Commission, the Federal Security Agency, the countless credit organizations of which former President Hoover has complained so bitterly, the Federal Deposit Insurance Corporation—are wide open to suggestions from the White House. And there is always the Presidency itself for men to rush to in the face of impending economic disaster.

There are limits, both strategic and physical, to what can be done in the White House, but certainly the alert President stands always ready to invite the managers of a sick industry or the leading citizens of a city plagued by chronic unemployment to come together and take counsel under his leadership. Of course, it is not his counsel but a well-placed government contract or a hike in the tariff or a dramatic recommendation to Congress that they have come for. Fortunately for the President, his position as overseer of the entire economy is obvious to even the most embittered spokesman for special interests, and he can take refuge from their pleas for relief by insisting that he must consider the whole picture before deciding on action in their behalf.

The very notion of the President as Manager of Prosperity is, for many people, an economic and political heresy. The tattered doctrine of the self-healing economy still claims the allegiance of several million Americans, who are especially vocal in the months before an election. Most of us, however, now accept the idea of a federal government openly engaged in preventing runaway booms and plunging busts. We need only think of Mr. Eisenhower's creditable performance in the slack days of 1954 to recognize the central position of the Presidency in this new kind of government. Lest there be any doubt how the President himself—this Republican President dedicated to the cause of free enterprise—feels about the new dimension of government responsibility, let me quote from his message to Congress accompanying the Economic Report for 1953:

The demands of modern life and the unsettled status of the world require a more important role for government than it played in earlier and quieter times. . . .

Government must use its vast power to help maintain employment and purchasing power as well as to maintain reasonably stable prices.

Government must be alert and sensitive to economic developments, including its own myriad activities. It must be prepared to take preventive as well as remedial action; and it must be ready to cope with new situations that may arise. This is not a start-and-stop responsibility, but a continuous one.

The arsenal of weapons at the disposal of Government for maintaining economic stability is formidable. It includes credit controls administered by the Federal Reserve System; the debt-management policies of the Treasury; authority of the President to vary the terms of mortgages carrying Federal insurance; flexibility in administration of the budget; agricultural supports; modification of the tax structure; and public works. We shall not hesitate to use any or all of these weapons as the situation may require.

In order to grasp the full import of the last of the President's roles, we must take him as Chief Diplomat, Commander in Chief, and Chief of State, then thrust him onto a far wider stage, there to perform before a much more numerous but no less critical audience. For the modern President is, whether we or our friends abroad like it or not, marked out for duty as the Leader of a Coalition of Free Nations, or at least as permanent presiding officer of various committees of his peers, the leaders of those nations united in the face of Soviet pressure. The President has a much larger constituency than the American electorate, for his words and deeds in behalf of our own survival as a free nation have a direct bearing upon the freedom and stability of at least a dozen, perhaps even two dozen other countries.

The reasons why he, rather than the British Prime Minister or French Premier or an outstanding figure from one of the smaller countries, should be singled out for supra-national leadership are too clear to require extended mention. Not only are we the richest and most powerful member of any coalition we may enter, not only are we the chief target of the enemy and thus the most truculent of the powers arrayed against him, but the Presidency, for the very reasons I have dwelled upon, unites power, drama, and prestige as does no other office in the world. Its incumbent sits, wherever he sits, at the head of the table. Winston Churchill, an A-plus student of our system of government, recognized this great truth with unerring eye when he insisted that not he, the elder statesman, but Mr. Eisenhower, the American President, take the chair in the middle at the Big Three conference in Bermuda in 1953. No British Prime Minister would ever be likely to forget that the President with whom he must deal every week of the year is a head of state as well as a head of government, a king and a prime minister rolled into one.

This role is not much more than a decade old, although there was a short rehearsal of it in late 1918 and the first few months of 1919. Whether it will continue to grow in the years of tension ahead depends, of course, on just how taut the tension remains. It does seem probable that the

President will have no choice but to act consciously for and speak openly to the nations with whom we are associated in defense of freedom—to act as Mr. Truman did in the North Korean aggression of June 1950, to speak as Mr. Eisenhower did in his proposal for an international atomic energy pool delivered to the Assembly of the United Nations in December 1953.

Having engaged in this piecemeal analysis of the Presidency, I hasten to fit the pieces back together into a seamless unity. For that, after all, is what the Presidency is, and I hope this exercise in political taxonomy has not obscured the paramount fact that it is a single office filled by a single man. I feel something like a professor of nutritional science who has just ticked off the ingredients of a wonderful stew. The members of the audience may be clear in their minds about the items in the pot, but they haven't the slightest notion of what the final product looks like or tastes like or will feel like in their stomachs. The Presidency, too, is a wonderful stew whose unique flavor cannot be accounted for simply by making a list of its ingredients. It is a whole greater than and different from the sum of its parts, an office whose power and prestige are something more than the arithmetical total of these ten functions. The President is not one kind of official one part of the day, another kind in another part— king in the morning, legislator at lunch, administrator in the afternoon, commander before dinner, and politician at odd moments that come his weary way. He is all these things all the time, and any one of his functions feeds upon and into all the others. He is a more exalted Chief of State because he is also Voice of the People, a more forceful Chief Diplomat because he commands the armed forces personally, a more effective Chief Legislator because the political system forces him to be Chief of Party, a more artful Manager of Prosperity because he is Chief Executive.

At the same time, several of these functions are plainly in competition, even in conflict, with one another, and not just in terms of their demands on the President's time and energy. The roles of Voice of the People and Chief of Party cannot both be played with equal fervor, as Mr. Truman proved on several occasions that had best be forgotten, while to act as Chief Diplomat but to think as Chief of Party, as Mr. Truman did in the Palestine crisis of 1948, can throw our foreign relations into indelicate confusion. Mr. Eisenhower certainly has had his periods in which, despite perfect health, he reigned too much and thus ruled too little, and one can think of several competent Presidents—Cleveland and Hoover, for example—who tried much too hard to be faithful Chief Executives.

There is no easy formula for solving this problem inherent in the nature of the office. If the Presidency is a chamber orchestra of ten pieces, all played by the leader, he must learn for himself by hard practice how to blend them together, remembering always that perfect harmony is unattainable, remembering, too, with Whitman, to "resist anything better than my own diversity." The only thing he can know for certain before he begins to make presidential music is that there are several parts—notably those of Chief of Party and Chief Administrator—that he must not play too long and loud lest he drown out the others.

The burden of these ten functions is colossal, and the President carries it as well as he does only because a remarkable array of administrative machinery has been invented to help him in his daily tasks, because

> Thousands at his bidding speed,
> And post o'er land and ocean without rest.

Yet the activities of this train of experts, the Executive Office and the Cabinet and all their offshoots and auxiliaries, must not draw our final attention away from the man all alone at the head. The Presidency, as I shall try to show in Chapter 4, has been converted into an institution during the past quarter-century, and we can never again talk about it sensibly without accounting for "the men around the President." Yet if it has become a twelve-hundred-man job in the budget and in the minds of students of public administration, it remains a one-man job in the Constitution and in the minds of the people—a truth of which we were dramatically reminded when the President fell ill in September 1955. Since it is a one-man job, the one man who holds it can never escape making the final decisions in each of the many areas in which the American people and their Constitution hold him responsible.

Mr. Truman, so it is said, used to keep a sign on his desk that read: "The buck stops here." That, in the end, is the essence of the Presidency. It is the one office in all the land whose occupant is forbidden to pass the buck.

CHAPTER 2

THE LIMITS OF THE PRESIDENCY

☆

The American Presidency is not universally admired. Most Americans think of it as a choice instrument of democratic government, but there are loud dissenters in this country, especially in deep right field, and sharp dissenters abroad, especially in those happy lands where the parliamentary system is counted a success. If the opinions of the former are generally too mixed up with politics to demand serious attention, the opinions of the latter deserve a hearing and rebuttal. The particulars of their bill of indictment against the Presidency read as follows:

1) The President and Congress, thanks chiefly to the independence that each enjoys under the Constitution, are set perennially at odds with one another. Antagonism is built into the system, and the President is forced willy-nilly to choose between meek withdrawal, which leaves the government leaderless, or bold aggression, which throws it into turmoil.

2) The President, thanks chiefly to his fixed term and his exemption from the final penalty of a vote of no confidence by the legislature, is held neither continuously responsible for his general conduct of office nor ever responsible for specific acts and policies. He feels not at all the kind of day-to-day, act-to-act accountability that compels the working head of government in a parliamentary system to mind every important step.

3) The Presidency, thanks to the whole of Article II of the Constitution, combines power and independence to a

dangerous degree. It is, indeed, a "matrix for dictatorship," as the Swiss took pains to point out while writing their Constitution of 1848. The sad history of the Presidency south of Florida and Texas is a warning to Americans that they had better think of reducing either the power or independence of the original model at home.

The American rebuttal to the case against the Presidency makes these general points: that it deals in a caricature of the real office, that it ignores the broad pattern of constitutional morality into which this office fits, and that its contempt for history is so flagrant as to raise laughs rather than doubts in our minds. More specifically, we reject the first particular by answering that the founding fathers "planned it that way," preferring imperfect safety to perfect efficiency, and that we their descendants are coming more and more to suspect that they wrought more shrewdly than they knew in separating the executive and legislative powers. Would this giant democracy of ours—spread over an entire continent, undisciplined by the sanctions of a clear-cut class structure, assaulted daily by the massed voices of vulgarity and unreason—make as safe and sane a success of parliamentary government as it seems to be making of our divided system? This is a question to which even the most perceptive of our home-grown constitutional reformers have yet to address themselves at all persuasively.

We reject the second particular not quite so confidently, for it would have been rather healthy, I think, to have held Mr. Roosevelt accountable for the "Court-packing" scheme, Mr. Truman for his proposed draft of the railroad strikers in 1946, and Mr. Eisenhower for the debacle over the Salk polio vaccine. But we cannot have the best of both great systems, and this—the too easy manner in which Presidents escape paying any real penalty for their blunders—is part of the minimum price we must meet in return for the benefits of the independent Presidency. And, after all, how do we know which kind of executive we would get if we were to adopt the parliamentary system in order to secure the blessings of continuous, piecemeal responsibility—the British Prime

Minister, who operates just about as freely as an executive should, or the French Premier, who is harassed at every step?

To the last criticism, that the Presidency blends too much power with too much independence, we can only make answer by pointing to the whole sweep of American political and constitutional history. Whatever grotesque shapes the Presidency may have assumed in Latin America, it has not been a matrix for dictatorship here in the United States, and I hardly think it an act of bravery, even an act of faith, to predict that it will not become one for a very long time, if ever. The Presidency, like every other instrument of power we have created for our use, operates within a grand and durable pattern of private liberty and public morality, which means that it operates successfully only when the President honors the pattern by selecting ends and means that are "characteristically American." I may well be accused of begging the question of dictatorship by saying that the American system simply would not permit it, but I know of no better way to underline the impossibility of our spawning and then succumbing to a Perón or a Batista than to point to the history and people of the United States and let it go at that.

The Presidency, be it noted, presents a most convincing argument in its own behalf and in that of the American people: 167 years, 33 Presidents, and still no despot or profligate or scoundrel has made the grade. In my opinion, no despot or profligate, and no scoundrel except Aaron Burr, ever made a good race, and perhaps the Presidency would have sobered even that "damaged soul." It was then and it is now the most thoroughly American of institutions, and I trust I will be excused from any further laboring of the plain historical and sociological truth that it is not a standing invitation to counterrevolution.

Yet, if we should not lose sleep over the possibility of a presidential *coup d'état,* we do have a right to worry about occasional abuses of power. The President is in a position to do serious damage, if not irreparable injury, to the ideals and methods of American democracy. Power that can be used decisively can also be abused grossly. No man can hold such a concentration of authority without feeling the urge, even though the urge be honest and patriotic, to push it beyond its usual bounds. We must therefore consider carefully the various safeguards that are counted upon to keep the President's feet in paths of constitutional righteousness. I have already discussed the powers of the President, as most writers on the subject delight to do, and now I think it proper to discuss the limits on him, as most do not. Blended together in judicious amounts, powers and limits make up a constitution, and the Presidency is nothing if not a constitutional office. Its powers are huge, but they are of no real effect— they are not, strictly speaking, powers at all—unless exercised through constitutional forms and within constitutional limits.

The search for limitations begins with the written and unwritten law, and thus with the Constitution. Like the good constitution it is, it grants spacious authority in a few frugal words—for which we must be ever grateful to the one-legged man who polished them so brightly—and then clamps on limitations with equal economy of detail. Restrictions on the President are sprinkled all through the Constitution. One has only to think of the rigid four-year term of office, the qualifications on the power of veto, and, to prove that we are not yet entirely content with the restrictions fixed by the framers, the flat ban on a third term established in the Twenty-second Amendment. Perhaps even more important than these specific restrictions are the powers the Constitution withholds silently from the President or bestows bountifully on other organs over which he has no control. The prime constitutional limit on the Presidency is the existence of Articles I and III.

The laws of Congress are full of implicit or explicit limitations. For one example, they rarely extend the President substantial authority today without requesting him to report to Congress on his use thereof annually or semiannually or at even briefer intervals. For another, he is limited sharply in his power of appointment by the many qualifications—as to citizenship, loyalty, political affiliations, professional attainments, residence, and the like—that the laws fix in varying degrees on "offices under the United States." The laws, like the Constitution, are full of indirect checks on the President, especially those statutes which set up agencies and commissions independent of his direction.

Like Congress and the justices themselves, the President can show eye-opening ingenuity in bypassing decisions of the Supreme Court. Yet no President can fail to recognize the restrictions set upon the free play of his executive will in *Humphrey's Executor* v. *U.S.* (1935), which upheld the power of Congress to protect certain administrative officials against arbitrary removal from office, and *Youngstown Sheet and Tube Co.* v. *Sawyer* (1952), which denied Mr. Truman authority to seize and operate the steel industry. Custom, too, can be ignored in unimportant matters and for short periods, but it has a way of asserting itself against the most strong-willed President. The ancient custom of Senatorial courtesy, which appears to have burst full-grown from the heads of the Senators from Georgia in the first year of Washington's administration, puts narrow limits on the President's power of appointment to hundreds of offices.

Most of these restrictions are fine and welcome, and they should be studied more thoughtfully by students of American government. Yet they exist on paper, and paper limitations, even those in the Constitution, need the support of living people and going institutions if they are to be of any force. We must therefore look further, into the political and social system all about us, if we are to learn what really puts the brakes on the President who has a mind to wander too far afield. "Brakes" is perhaps not the happiest word to use in this instance, because I am concerned with persons and institutions and centers of power that not only block the President's way, convincing him that a course of action is more trouble than it is worth or even frustrating him flatly, but often force him to take a course of action that he does not want to take at all. What are some of these, and how do they operate to restrain or persuade him?

The first and most vigorous is the Congress of the United States—a concourse of self-willed persons, a truly venerable institution, a fiercely independent center of power. Some of the weapons with which it may check or persuade the President are bright with use; others have not been hauled out and brandished for many years. Yet all must be reckoned with by any President who sets out upon an extraordinary line of conduct or tries to run away and hide from conflict. Let me list them briefly and add one or two comments.

The power of legislation is one that I have already touched upon sufficiently by indicating some of the ways in which the President is limited by statute. I would add only the observation that this power is a great deal easier for Congress to wield over future Presidents than over the President of the moment. Yet the Humphrey-Stennis resolution of July 1955, which set up the Wright Commission to investigate and report on the loyalty and security program, shows that pressure can sometimes be applied by law to an incumbent President. A shrewdly designed statute persuaded Mr. Eisenhower much against his stated will to join in re-examining a program for which he was primarily responsible. Another statutory check, whose potentialities have yet to be fully explored, is the provision occasionally inserted in broad delegations of emergency power that permits the power to be recaptured by concurrent resolution, that is, without the President's consent. In addition, many grants of power are made for limited periods; some of the most important wartime statutes named specific terminal dates. And there is always the "rider" placed artfully in a bill the President cannot afford to veto. Rutherford B. Hayes, I am told by residents of Fremont, Ohio, still shakes in his grave every time a President is forced to protest against this practice.

The power of investigation, which includes the power to ask questions and get answers from the President's chief lieutenants, calls for even less comment. The excellent uses and disgraceful abuses of this power over the past two decades are etched sharply in our memories, and it is scarcely necessary to point out that in many of the leading investigations of this period—those, for example, conducted by Senator McCarthy in 1953 and Senator Kefauver in 1955—the real target was the President himself. While these men were engaged in high theater, other congressmen, less ambitious and more merciful, were plodding quietly ahead with the routine inquiries into administrative purposes, methods, and shortcomings that do much to keep the Chief Executive and his helpers in touch with democratic realities.

The power of the purse was once upon a time considered the most formidable of Congress's weapons, and there are those who persist in talking about it as did Madison in *The Federalist*:

This power over the purse may, in fact, be regarded as the most complete and effectual weapon with which any constitution can arm the immediate representatives of the people, for obtaining a redress of every grievance, and for carrying into effect every just and salutary measure.

I am afraid we must enter a dissent to this much too optimistic and mechanical evaluation of the "power over the purse." Instances in which Congress slapped a President, and hurt him, by withholding funds from schemes in which he had an intense personal interest do not come to mind in bunches. Perhaps the most notable use of this power in recent years was the senseless murder of the National Resources Planning Board in 1943 by the Seventy-eighth Congress. In the same year, however, Mr. Roosevelt sent in a budget of $100,000,000,000, and Congress fell all over itself trying to give the Commander in Chief everything he needed to win the war—everything, that is, but the National Resources Planning Board. In the warfare-welfare state, which Madison could hardly have foreseen, the power of the purse exists more in rhetoric than in fact. Indeed, the evidence is rather convincing that in time of emergency, when controls on expenditures are most needed, Congress itself takes the lead in loosening them.

⟶ The power of impeachment is the extreme medicine of the Constitution, so extreme—and so brutally administered in the one instance in which it was prescribed for a President—that most observers now agree with Jefferson that it is a "mere scare-crow" and with Henry Jones Ford that it is a "rusted blunderbuss, that will probably never be taken in hand again." Yet the power is there, imbedded adamantly in the Constitution, and it could yet be wielded over a President who engages openly in "treason, bribery, or other high crimes and misdemeanors." If it is not, as Professor Edward S. Corwin has written, "an effective weapon in the arsenal of liberty," this must be largely due "to the fact that Presidents have in the past kept pretty clear of courses which might make people think seriously of so extreme a discipline." I predict confidently that the next President to be impeached will have asked for the extreme medicine by committing a low personal rather than a high political crime—by shooting a Senator, for example.

Finally, Congress, or either house, retains the power of "soft impeachment," although this, too, has been used on a President only about once a century. The Senate's censure of Andrew Jackson in 1834 for "the late executive proceedings in relation to the public revenue" was the most drastic exercise of this extraordinary power. It cannot be said to have had much influence on Jackson's subsequent conduct; rather, it proved to be one of the most deadly boomerangs in American political history. An interesting variation on the power of censure was the resolution of the Republican conferences in the House and Senate in December 1950 demanding the removal of Secretary of State Acheson. This unprecedented "vote of no confidence" by the minority party may have hurt Mr. Acheson's prestige at the Brussels parley, but it, too, proved a boomerang. One suspects that nothing short of a gun at his head, and perhaps not even that, could thereafter have persuaded Mr. Truman to throw his Secretary of State from the sleigh to the Republican wolves.

The real power of Congress to check or persuade a President lies in none of the positive weapons I have just reviewed, for the real power of Congress over him is essentially negative in character. Two points are worth remembering in this connection: first, that no great policy, domestic or foreign, can be maintained effectively by a President without the approval of Congress in the form of laws and money; and second, that there is no way under our Constitution for a President to force Congress to pass a law or spend money against its will. In the course of this book I have several times pointed with pride and awe to the unique independence of our executive, but I could also have pointed—with no less pride and perhaps more awe—to the unique independence of our legislature. If the members of Congress cannot force the President to resign by a vote of no confidence, neither can he dissolve Congress. If his term is rigidly fixed, so, too, is theirs. Ours is just about the only legislature in the world over whose decisions the executive has no final power of persuasion, either in political fact or constitutional theory. He has *influence,* and the influence may be great— as Franklin Roosevelt proved in March 1933—but he has no *power.* Nor is the indissolubility of Congress the only bulwark of its independence. It, too, draws its authority directly from the Constitution; it, too, arises out of a constituency essentially its own.

Let me illustrate this point with the aid of a passage from Beard's *Republic.* The Glaucon of the piece, Dr. Smyth, has just made a sweeping assertion of presidential power in foreign affairs—something like the one I made in the first chapter—and Socrates, Professor Beard, is not the man to let him get away with it:

Now let me put some yes or no questions to you, the kind you like to put to me. Can the President alone regulate intercourse with other countries at his pleasure—that is, tariffs, tonnage duties, financial exchanges, and travel?

No. Congress has that power.

Can the President at his pleasure regulate immigration and emigration?

No. Congress passes immigration acts.

Can the President determine the conditions of naturalization and the rights of aliens in the United States?

No.

Can the President fix the size and nature of our army, navy, and other armed forces?

No.

Can the President alone set up ministries and consulates in other countries and pick his own ministers and consuls?

No. Since Congress must provide the money for them, it could control this branch of foreign business, if it wanted to do so. Besides, the Senate must approve the persons named by the President as ministers or ambassadors.

Can the President make treaties with other countries?

No. A treaty must have the approval of two-thirds of the Senate. But the President can make minor agreements without asking the consent of the Senate.

Can the President declare war?

No. That power is supposed to be in the hands of Congress.

Can the President make peace?

If it takes a treaty, the Senate must approve.

Can the President declare the foreign policy of the United States and impose it on the country by his own will?

There are two questions. Certainly the President can declare the foreign policy of the United States. But he cannot impose it upon the country by mere declaration.

There is more of this kind of talk, but the passage will suffice to remind us of the President's reliance on Congress for support of even his most splendid prerogatives.

I could proceed indefinitely discussing this most crucial relationship in our system of government. For example, I should say something about the three negative powers of the Senate, two of which it draws from the Constitution, the third of which it has bestowed upon its own grateful self: 1) the power of a majority to withhold consent from the President's nominations; 2) the power of one-third (plus one) "of the Senators present" to withhold consent from the treaties he submits to it; and 3) the power of a "little group of willful men, representing no opinion but their own," to hamstring the desire of a majority of both houses to give the President a grant of authority or money for which he may have desperate need. Some of the most celebrated filibusters in the Senate's history have been directed against the policies and even the person of a President. I should also say something about the way in which committees of Congress, not to mention strong-willed individuals, wield persuasive power over administrators and thus indirectly over the President. Yet I trust I have made my point with sufficient vigor: the most reliable single limitation on the American Presidency is the independent existence of a proud, jealous, watchful co-ordinate branch. No President ever lived who would not have agreed, reverently or ruefully, with this statement.

The restricting powers of the third independent branch are a delusive shadow compared with the sweep of authority just reviewed. For most practical purposes, the President may act as if the Supreme Court did not exist. It takes a raw action by an imprudent President to invite judicial condemnation, and most exertions of executive power, however raw, are directed to questions over which no court would presume to exercise the slightest measure of supervision or even judgment.

This is especially true of the President's activities in time of war, as one may read for himself in the *United States Reports* published during and after our three great conflicts. At the very moment when the President, whether Lincoln or Wilson or Roosevelt, was drawing most audaciously on the Commander-in-Chief clause for authority to regulate the lives and property of the people, the Court was drawing most sheepishly on its bag of tricks to avoid a showdown with him and his military subordinates. The reason for excessive judicial self-restraint in time of war is, of course, obvious and compelling: a challenge in court to an evacuation order or a plant seizure or a suspension of the writ of habeas corpus raises a question so politically explosive, perhaps so vital to national survival, that the very notion of "government by lawsuit" becomes unthinkable. Whatever we allow this process to settle in time of peace, we cannot submit to its vagaries in time of war—a truth that the Court itself has been the first to acknowledge by avoiding unfavorable judgments on the President's orders as Commander in Chief. Like Congress's power of the purse, the Court's power of judicial review is least useful when most needed.

Yet the Court does own a few spectacular victories over the President. Several of these, like *Humphrey's Executor* v. *U.S.* (1935), came too late to be of much use or warning to anyone involved. The most famous and confidently quoted of all limiting decisions, *Ex parte Milligan* (1866), was announced a full year after the assassination of the President who was being censured—in this instance for authorizing the trial of civilians by military commission in an area far removed from the theater of war. Cases like *Schecter Bros.* v. *U.S.* (1934) and *Youngstown Sheet and Tube Co.* v. *Sawyer* (1952), however, brought down high-flying Presidents at the top of their trajectories. Whatever else may be said of the Schecter case, which cut the legal ground from under the National Recovery Administration, it was a healthy exhibition of constitutional government in action, and it was the President, not the Court, who took the crucial step by ordering the N.R.A. to fold its tents without delay. The Steel Seizure case was an equally dramatic vindication of constitutional practice, and again it was the President who bowed deeply, if hardly reverently, to constituted authority by ordering the Secretary of Commerce to relinquish possession of the steel mills.

In neither of these cases was the President himself before the Court. Jefferson's rejection of Marshall's *subpoena duces tecum* in the Burr trial and Chase's opinion in *Mississippi* v. *Johnson* (1867), which spared Andrew Johnson the necessity of answering a writ of injunction, make clear that the judiciary has no power to enjoin or mandamus or even question the President. His subordinates, however, do not share his immunity from the judicial process. Whenever a claim or justification is based on the authority of a presidential order, the order itself may come under challenge in the form of a suit against those seeking to enforce it. The interesting old case of *Little* v. *Barreme* (1804) presents one clear-cut instance

in which the Court held a presidential order to be without
legal warrant; *Panama Refining Co.* v. *Ryan* (1934) presents
another.

I do not wish to sound too harsh or hopeless in my final
estimate of the Court as a restraint on presidential power.
No one can doubt the high moral standing of a case like
Humphrey's Executor v. *U.S.,* least of all some future President who decides to stir up the hornets by removing a commissioner from one of the independent agencies. Even as
he chooses a course of action that permits him to ignore
Justice Sutherland's opinion in that case, he will have to explain carefully to Congress and people, and in time to the
Court, just what distinguishes this removal from that effected
by Franklin Roosevelt in 1934. Yet we would be deluding ourselves cruelly if we were to count on the Court to save us
from the consequences of an abuse of presidential power.
The fact is that the Court has done more over the years to
expand than to contract the authority of the Presidency—
as witness the *Prize Cases* (1863), in which it supported Lincoln's blockade of the South; *In re Debs* (1895), in which it
approved Cleveland's strong line of action in the Pullman
strike; *United States* v. *Curtiss-Wright Export Corp.* (1936),
in which it spoke glowingly of the President's power in
foreign relations; and the long series of cases in which it
purified and strengthened the powers to pardon offenses and
veto bills. In the nature of things judicial and political, the
Court can be expected to go on rationalizing most pretensions
of most Presidents. It is clearly one of the least reliable restraints on presidential activity.

A more reliable restraint is to be found in the federal administration—in the persons and politics and prejudices of,
let us say, the top twenty thousand civil and military officials
of the government of the United States. Were the Presidents
of the last fifty years to be polled on this question, all but one
or two, I am sure, would agree that the "natural obstinacy"
of the average bureau chief or commissioner or colonel was
second only to the "ingrained suspicions" of the average

congressman as a check on the President's ability to do either good or evil. Several would doubtless go further to insist that the President's hardest job is, not to persuade Congress to support a policy dear to his political heart, but to persuade the pertinent bureau or agency—even when headed by men of his own choosing—to follow his direction faithfully and transform the shadow of the policy into the substance of a program. No President, they would tell us sadly, can accomplish anything lasting in influence without the energetic assistance of a whole train of civil servants, most of whom were on the job long before he arrived and will be there long after he has departed. In seeking to win this kind of assistance, in trying to "get on top and stay on top" of his administration or even a part of it, a President could easily dissipate all his time, energy, and capacity for leadership.

This is not to say that the federal administration is led and staffed by men whose one purpose in life is to ignore, emasculate, or otherwise frustrate the legitimate wishes of the President. Quite the contrary, our federal civil servants are no less anxious than he to get on with the business of good and democratic government. But his idea and their idea of what is "good" or "democratic" must often be at stiff odds with one another, especially when he is pushing some untried and unconventional policy, even more especially when they have the support of strong men and groups in Congress. It is too much to expect, short of the kind of drastic therapy or surgery that may well leave an agency in no condition to act at all, that such a policy can be the same in execution as it was in conception. I think, in this instance, of all the written and spoken directives of our last three Presidents aimed at eliminating racial discrimination in the civil service and the armed forces, and I wonder how many thousands of times some stubborn or fainthearted official has made a mockery of the President's good intentions. I think, too, of the trials undergone by Truman and Eisenhower in persuading certain chiefs of staff to shape their acts and speeches to the policies of the administration. At the same time, we may take comfort in the thought that the traditions of our armed forces would forbid support of a President in a *coup d'état*.

I shall have more to say about the President's difficulties as an administrator in later chapters. Here I need only call attention to certain broad features of the administrative branch that can be counted on to hobble a crusading President—even when the crusade is obviously launched against the forces of darkness. The first of these is the mere size of the federal administration, which now makes it impossible for a President to know or see or influence personally more than a handful of those men whose day-to-day activities will determine whether some cherished policy is to succeed or fail. What Burke said of the old British Empire, we may say of the new American government: "In large bodies, the circulation of power must be less vigorous at the extremities. Nature has said it." At many extremities of the federal administration the circulation of presidential power cannot be felt at all.

The second feature is pluralism in law, and a close corollary is pluralism in fact. Many agencies are rendered independent of the President's immediate supervision by statute; many more are exempt from his influence because of political and personal circumstances. The most usual circumstance, one that can frustrate any President, is that of an upright agency headed by a case-hardened chief who numbers more real friends among the leaders of Congress than any President who ever lived, not even excluding William G. McKinley. The Federal Bureau of Investigation under J. Edgar Hoover, the Passport Office under Mrs. Ruth Shipley and Miss Frances Knight, and the Corps of Engineers under almost anyone are examples of what I mean by "pluralism in fact." Although a President may count on these agencies to execute the laws faithfully according to their own lights, he would invite disaster, both administrative and political, if he tried to alter the course that each has been following for these many years. Mr. Hoover has a kind of tenure that even the most carefully sheltered administrator should have reason to envy; his time-tested ability to outlast the President of the moment must always give that President pause. I cannot help wondering how often President Truman thought of relieving Mr. Hoover—and then thought a second time, sighed, and went about his business.

Finally, I need only mention such qualities of any administration as tradition, pride, inertia, and professional knowledge and competence to show that the President, be his intentions good or bad, is checked sharply by the mere existence of all those thousands of top-grade public servants over whom he simply cannot expect to have the control in fact that he does in law, and of those hundreds over whom he has no effective control at all. Nor does it afford him much comfort to know that he hires and fires the men on top of the executive departments, for few of these are his unquestioning supporters and all must suffer the existence of bureau and division heads who make their own deals with congressional committees for power, funds, and prestige. There are more programs under way in the federal administration than any one President has ever dreamed of initiating, terminating, or bending to his will.

Another series of restraints upon the President arises out of our political system, by which I mean the two major parties. We all know well the many ways in which the leaders of the opposition party can make hash of his plans and a misery of his existence. They can badger his assistants, investigate his methods, vote down his requests, question his motives, keep a record of the times he plays golf, and, as in the congressional elections of 1918 and 1946, beat him in the process of beating his party at the polls. If the President is the grand sachem of his own party and thus the symbol of its hopes and instrument of its principles, the party that fought him tooth and nail at his election must continue to fight him, with perhaps a little more restraint now that he is President, all through his four years in office. His record is essentially the record of his party, and the party in opposition, which wants desperately to put its own man in the White House, cannot be expected to let him have his own way except in matters that touch upon our survival as a nation. Even as he struggles with these matters he will be harassed by the enemy's irregulars. The most effective check of all in our system of checks and balances is one the framers themselves tried to save us from with all their skill—the party in opposition, which now means the party that lost the Presidency in the last election. No party can think of itself as the governing party in this country unless it can claim the authority and prestige of the White House.

If the opposing party is a roadblock in the path of the President, his own party is at best a drag. He draws great power from his position as Chief of Party, but with it comes the obligation to work and live with the men who elected him to office. Not only must he be careful not to plunge too far ahead or lag too far to the rear of his allies in Congress; he must pay homage to the traditions of the party, select his chief lieutenants from its ranks, act as "honest broker" among its squabbling wings, and endure silently attacks upon his integrity by men who roam the outer reaches of party loyalty. In doing all these things for the sake of harmony, and for the sake of victory in the next election, he cannot help losing some of his zest for bold experiment. In most instances that matter he must work with the party or not at all. The party, as we know from the history of a dozen administrations, is more likely to tame him than he is to reshape it. Franklin Roosevelt, supposedly the most dominant of political leaders, felt the drag of his own party through most of his years in office. The Democrats on the House Rules Committee and Senate Judiciary Committee, not the Republicans huddled together in the Cave of Adullam, were the impenetrable barrier between him and some of his most ardently sought goals. And even Mr. Eisenhower, who has little taste for adventure, has been hampered rather than invigorated by his leadership of the Republican party. The party that makes him also brakes him—this is the lot, not entirely unhappy, of the modern President.

When we look beyond the national government and the parties that are its lifeblood, we note at least three other centers or dispersions of power that stand in the President's way and often force him to take troublesome detours. The first of these is the federal system—an involved network of forty-eight separate and independent governments and their countless subdivisions, all of which possess powers whose use or disuse can seriously embarrass the President and his policies. Although the states no longer have the restraining influence of the days when they defied Jefferson, ignored Madison, and heckled Lincoln, they remain an obstacle to the determined President, especially to one who is eager to push ahead boldly with experiments in education and racial justice. In conducting foreign relations, too, the President may discover that the states still hold some power to irritate if not to persuade him. In 1906 Theodore Roosevelt's Japanese policy nearly foundered on the anti-Oriental obstinacy of the San Francisco Board of Education; the Board gave way to the President only after he had promised to see what he could do to reduce the flow of Japanese immigrants into California. In 1913 the Republican-dominated legislature of California made even more trouble for President Wilson by passing an alien land law aimed primarily at the Japanese—despite the earnest pleas of the President, which Secretary of State Bryan delivered personally in Sacramento, that the nation be spared the consequences of this insult to proud Japan.

Far stronger than the states as a check on the Presidency is the American system of free enterprise—that fabulous galaxy of corporations, small businesses, partnerships, individual enterprises, trade associations, co-operatives, unions, consumer groups, and foundations through which the power of economic decision is splintered and diffused in the interest of freedom and progress. The President must enlist a great deal of private support among both management and labor if he is to make his authority as Manager of Prosperity felt in the face of impending economic disaster. His bid for support may often be spurned by some group of men in the economy who just do not want to be managed into prosperity, at least prosperity as he defines it.

And he can be spurned—no doubt of that. There have been several occasions in recent years when free enterprise, or even a single free enterpriser, has defied a President with impunity and even brought him to terms. John L. Lewis, the last of the robber barons, has driven at least three Presidents to consider either homicide or suicide, and Clarence Randall may be remembered most vividly for his televised attack on President Truman's order to seize the steel industry in April 1952. Mr. Randall's opening and closing words on that occasion are well worth recording, for they give a candid picture of an American mind wrestling with the prickly truth that the political head of government is also the ceremonial head of state:

> I have a deep sense of responsibility as I face this vast audience of the air. I am here to make answer on behalf of the steel industry to charges flung over these microphones last night by the man who then stood where I stand now. I am a plain citizen. He was the President of the United States.
>
> Happily we still live in a country where a private citizen may look the President in the eye and tell him that he was wrong, but actually it is not the President of the United States to whom I make answer.
>
> It is Harry S. Truman, the man, who last night so far transgressed his oath of office, so far abused the power which is temporarily his, that he must now stand and take it.
>
> I shall not let my deep respect for the office which he holds stop me from denouncing his shocking distortions of fact. Nor shall I permit the honor of his title to blind the American people from the enormity of what he has done.
>
> He has seized the steel plants of the nation, the private property of one million people, most of whom now hear the sound of my voice. This he has done without the slightest shadow of legal right. . . .
>
> For whom has he done this? Let no American be misled. This evil deed, without precedent in American history, discharges a political debt to the C.I.O. Phil Murray now gives Harry S. Truman a receipt marked "paid in full." I present this forthright reply to the President only because I believe deeply in the truth of what I have said. I should feel derelict in my own duty as a citizen if I did not tonight call upon Americans everywhere to take up the challenge the President threw down last night.

Whereupon Mr. Randall and his associates took up the challenge themselves and, eight weeks later, drove the President and Secretary of Commerce Sawyer headlong from their mills. Their troubles were far from over, but they had defeated a President in a battle of his choosing.

I have already referred to the President's obligations to his colleagues and constituents overseas. No obligation that goes with this new dimension of leadership is more certain and pressing than his duty to listen carefully, and pay heed when he can, to the suggestions of our friends throughout the world, for on these terms alone can we maintain the alliances upon which we depend for survival as a self-governing people. This means, of course, that in shaping a military or foreign policy the President must give careful thought to how persons outside as well as inside the country will respond. He must henceforth sense a reduction in his freedom to conduct the delicate business of diplomacy and the nasty business of war because of pressures flowing from London and Paris and Tokyo, as well as from New Delhi and the United Nations building in New York. Dozens of times since World War II our Presidents have acted as they have because Sir Winston Churchill or Sir Anthony Eden or M. Mendès-France or, let us not forget, Syngman Rhee has persuaded them to act that way. Would Mr. Eisenhower have gone to the Summit in July 1955 if he had not been entreated by Eden and Premier Faure? And would Sir Anthony have entreated quite so persuasively had he not been faced with a general election, one that Mr. Eisenhower had a strong desire to see him win? It would seem that the people as well as the political leaders of other nations can occasionally speed a President up or slow him down.

This brings me to the last and, over the long run, most effective check upon the President: the opinions of the people of the United States, which our pressure groups can be counted on to express with zeal. Lincoln is supposed to have said that he could do anything with "public sentiment" but nothing without it or against it; and if he did not say it, we can say it for him. The President draws immense authority from the support of the American people, but only if he uses it in ways they understand and approve, which generally means ways that are fair, dignified, traditional, and familiar. He can lead public opinion, but only so far as public opinion is willing to go, and it is splendidly inert on dozens of great issues. He can steer it a bit, too, and occasionally redirect its course, but he cannot make it take a direction that goes against what I have called our "grand and durable pattern of private liberty and public morality." For if he flouts either the considered judgments or ill-considered prejudices of any vocal segment of the people, if he chances to roam too far outside the accepted limits of presidential behavior, he will find himself exposed to all those enemies who multiply like mosquitoes in a Jersey August whenever a President plays the game too hard. No President, certainly no peacetime President, ever wielded more power with less need to worry about the political consequences than did Franklin Roosevelt in 1933, yet even then the assumption was abroad that there were some steps he could not take, some measures he could not recommend to Congress, in his effort to rescue "a stricken Nation in the midst of a stricken world." Let me drive this point home with a few words from a devoted admirer of the President, Professor Harold Laski, who wanted a new deck more than a New Deal:

> Vast innovations for which the public is unprepared are almost bound to fail, because they are almost certain to shock. There can be experiment in the tactics of policy; there can hardly, without great danger, be experiment in fundamental ideas. Those observers who say that Mr. Roosevelt missed a great opportunity in 1933 when he did not nationalize the banking system seem to me wholly to misconceive the nature of the presidential office. While it was possible that, at that grave moment, the president might have carried through such a scheme, it was so widely outside the range of common expectation that it would have destroyed his authority for the rest of his term in office. Nothing in previous discussion had prepared the public for such a measure. Nothing in the electoral conception of Mr. Roosevelt had prepared the public to associate him with such a strategy. He might have won the battle; he would have lost the campaign.

Thinking of Mr. Roosevelt's defeat in his fight to enlarge the Supreme Court in 1937, I would go a step beyond Laski and assert that he would not even have won the battle. Public opinion in this country in 1933, or at least the opinion of a large and dogged segment of it, would never have made peace with the idea of nationalizing the banking system, and it would surely have found a dozen ways to harry the President into surrender. These ways still exist and have, if anything, grown stronger in the past twenty years. And by "ways" I do not mean simply such outlets for American opinion as radio, television, Gallup and Roper polls, letters to the White House, or even elections, useful as all these may be as storm warnings to a President. The real force of public opinion as a limit on the Presidency is felt through the other restraints I have described in this chapter. Public opinion, that is to say, works most effectively on a President when it encourages Congress to override a veto, persuades an investigating committee to put a White House intimate on the grill, stiffens the resolve of a band of Senators to talk until Christmas, convinces an ousted commissioner that his ouster is worth fighting in the courts, and puts backbone in a Supreme Court asked to nullify a presidential order. The various institutions and centers of power that check the President are inept and often useless without public opinion—and with it wondrously armed.

All this is especially true of Congress, which never feels that life is so worth living as when it condemns the President or refuses to grant his request for power because it senses that for once it, not he, has "rightly interpreted the national thought." If he tries to persuade Congress improperly or pushes ahead in defiance of all the rules, he invites the one disaster from which Presidents rarely recover: the loss of genuine popular support.

In the end, of course, the checks that hold the President in line are internal rather than external. His conscience and training, his sense of history and desire to be judged well by it, his awareness of the need to pace himself lest he collapse under the burden—all join to halt him far short of the kind of deed that destroys a President's "fame and power." He, like the rest of us, has been raised in the American tradi-

tion; he, perhaps better than the rest of us, senses what the
tradition permits and what it forbids in the conduct of high
office. If he knows anything of history or politics or administration, he knows that he can do great things only within
"the common range of expectation," that is to say, in ways
that honor or at least do not outrage the accepted dictates of
constitutionalism, democracy, personal liberty, and Christian
morality.

And so we return to the point from which we set forth on
this journey around the perimeter of presidential power,
and again I beg the question of dictatorship by saying that
the American system would not permit it. This republic has
had its share of "God's angry men," and some of them have
climbed up to high places and set off damaging explosions.
But none has even got a good start on the climb to the highest
place of all. Our political rules demand categorically that
a candidate for the Presidency be, first, a politician able to
unite a party in whose house there are a hundred mansions,
and, second, a statesman able to bid confidently for the
votes of a majority of the American constituency. It has un-
failing ways of singling out and rejecting the man who cannot
do these things because he is too angry or anxious or un-
principled. Men like Thaddeus Stevens and Huey Long and
Senator McCarthy may wield vast powers of provocation
and intimidation in their time, but no party with the faint-
est hope of winning the big election will ever nominate such
a man to lead it. I think a good test of a man's understanding
of the American system was his recognition, even in 1952 and
1953, that Senator McCarthy might help to make or break
a President but could never be one himself. At least one of
Hamilton's confident observations in *The Federalist* still
rings true:

> The process of election affords a moral certainty, that the office of
> President will never fall to the lot of any man who is not in an eminent
> degree endowed with the requisite qualifications. Talents for low in-
> trigue, and the little arts of popularity, may alone suffice to elevate
> a man to the first honors in a single state; but it will require other

talents, and a different kind of merit, to establish him in the esteem and confidence of the whole Union, or of so considerable a portion of it as would be necessary to make him a successful candidate for the distinguished office of President of the United States. It will not be too strong to say, that there will be a constant probability of seeing the station filled by characters preeminent for ability and virtue.

Or at least by characters with enough ability to lead an American-style party and enough virtue to appeal to a majority of one of the world's most enlightened electorates.

Let me refix attention upon the President who is already in office, upon the one, if it please, in office at the moment of writing. Like all our Presidents, he is quite unlikely to hazard a dictatorship; but, again like all of them, he is quite likely to indulge in occasional misuses of power. My concern has been to describe the network of restraints that keeps him from indulging too often and too perniciously in such misuses, and I think it essential to round off this description with two observations. First, no one of these massive centers of power—Congress, Court, administration, parties, states, economy, people—operates alone in restraining him. They form, as I have said, a network, and the strength of the network arises from the interlocking of all its parts. One fortifies the other and is in turn fortified by it. A genuinely indecent performance by the President will arouse fierce opposition in every part of our system, and even a questionable course of action, such as Mr. Eisenhower's series of blunders in the Dixon-Yates affair, will move congressmen, administrators, lobbyists, and politicians to unite in opposition. Several observers were moved to remark in the midst of that controversy that the President seemed never to have heard of John C. Calhoun's doctrine of the "concurrent majority," or surely he would have realized that no important program can be brought off in this country without the concurrence of a clear majority of the social and economic interests with a stake in the outcome. One always had the feeling that Mr. Eisenhower would lose in the end—if not the battle, certainly the campaign. And when he did lose the battle, he lost not only to the city of Memphis but to a whole host of other interests that had fought him implacably on a dozen fronts. There are those, to be sure, who think of the Dixon-Yates contract as a proper agreement properly made, which is as useful a thought as any to illustrate the truth that the system can prevent a President from doing good as well as evil. In the end, however, we must hold fast to the faith, which is surely borne out by history, that the network of restraints on the President works about as well as we have a right to expect our institutions to work. Much, after all, is left to chance among free men. As we cannot expect power to be used only to do good, so we cannot expect limitations to be used only to block evil.

My second point is that the President is not a Gulliver, immobilized by ten thousand tiny cords, nor even a Prometheus, chained to a rock of frustration. He is, rather, a kind of magnificent lion who can roam widely and do great deeds so long as he does not try to break loose from his broad reservation. Our pluralistic system of restraints is designed to keep him from going out of bounds, not to paralyze him in the field that has been reserved for his use. He will feel few checks upon his power if he uses that power as he should. This may well be the final definition of the strong and successful President: the one who knows just how far he can go in the direction he wants to go. If he cannot judge the limits of his power, he cannot call upon its strength. If he cannot sense the possible, he will exhaust himself attempting the impossible. The power of the Presidency moves as a mighty host only *with* the grain of liberty and morality.

CHAPTER 3

THE PRESIDENCY IN HISTORY

☆

The roots of the American Presidency run deep into history. In a world in which model constitutions with their model executives have come and gone in profusion over the past 150 years, this office stands forth as a truly venerable institution. We cannot take its full measure unless we know something of its history, and its history, in any case, is worth studying for its own exciting sake. With no further ado I plunge headlong into it.

The point of origin to which I would first direct attention is the Constitutional Convention of 1787, although like all such points it had origins of its own—in this instance far back in English constitutional history. To understand the kind of executive created in Article II of the Constitution, we must know something of the men who wrote it, the purposes they had in mind, the materials with which they worked, and the experience that was their final guide.

The men most influential in shaping the Presidency were James Wilson, who campaigned tirelessly for an executive that could operate with "energy, dispatch, and responsibility"; James Madison, who swung around slowly, but in the end decisively, to Wilson's advanced yet sensible views; and Gouverneur Morris, who led the battle for an energetic executive on the floor of the Convention and then sealed the victory by writing the final draft of the Constitution. Hamilton and Washington, too, each in his own way, deserve some credit for the original Presidency.

The purposes of all these men were the purposes of the

whole Convention: to rescue the new republic from the turbulent aftermath of revolution by establishing a new government with sufficient energy to insure domestic tranquillity, secure the blessings of ordered liberty, protect private property, create conditions favorable to commercial prosperity, gain respect for itself and fair treatment for its citizens abroad, unite the states in pursuit of common ends, and return the reins of power to the "enlightened gentry." Men like Wilson and Morris understood more clearly than men like Roger Sherman and Edmund Randolph that a strong and independent executive was an essential element of any such government.

The materials with which they worked were the colonial governorships and thus, more remotely, the British monarchy; the various solutions to the problem of executive power in the first state constitutions; the administrative departments that had developed under the Articles of Confederation; and the writings of such exponents of balanced government as Locke and Montesquieu. The experience, both happy and unhappy, of the leaders of the Convention finally dictated the choice of the New York Constitution of 1777 and the Massachusetts Constitution of 1780 as the chief materials. The contrast between these two states, where independent executives served the cause of stability and order, and states like North Carolina and Rhode Island, where unchecked legislatures engaged in all sorts of unseemly activities, did not escape the attention of the delegates at Philadelphia. They had had their fill of governments, both state and national, in which "everything has been drawn within the legislative vortex." Between 1776 and 1787 there had been a noticeable shift in the constitutional theory of the moderate Whigs from whose ranks came the framers of the Constitution—a shift away from innate confidence in popular assemblies and toward the suspicion that, as Jefferson wrote in his *Notes on Virginia,* "173 despots would surely be as oppressive as one." The sharp decline in the prestige of Congress and the state assemblies among conservatives throughout the new republic was a major factor in the decision to adopt a form of government in which the legislature would be balanced by a strong executive, not mismatched with a "mere Cipher."

The progress of the Convention toward this decision was labored and uncertain, however, and it often seemed that the hard lessons of the previous decade would be wasted on a majority of the delegates. Persistent voices were raised against almost every arrangement that eventually appeared in Article II, and Wilson and his colleagues were able to score their final success only after a series of debates, decisions, reconsiderations, references to committees, and private maneuvers that still leave the historian befuddled. I have followed the tortuous progress of the incipient Presidency through Madison's *Notes* four times, and I am still not sure how the champions of the strong executive won their smashing victory. It can be said for certain, however, that at least eight decisions on the structure and powers of the executive were taken at different stages of the proceedings, and that out of these arose the Presidency. Every one of these decisions, with one partial exception that history was shortly to remedy, was taken in favor of a strong executive. The consequences for the Presidency, indeed for our whole system of government, would have been enormous had any one of them been taken differently—as it could easily have been. Let me list these decisions briefly, first giving notice that this list lends a deceptive appearance of order to a highly disordered train of events:

1) An executive would be established separate from the legislature. Although this was surely the easiest of all eight decisions to adopt, there were those like Sherman who continued to wonder aloud if it would not be wiser to leave the legislature free to create and appoint such executives "as experience might dictate." To most delegates it was clear from the outset that the executive should be created in the Constitution itself. This had not been done in the first American constitution, and most hardheaded patriots considered this one of the serious defects in the Articles of Confederation.

2) The executive would consist of one man, a President of the United States. This fateful decision was taken only after considerable debate, and only after Wilson had used his position as chairman of the Committee on Detail to spike the plans of those like Randolph who feared the one-man executive as a "foetus of monarchy." Had Randolph and his friends had their way, the Presidency, or whatever it might have been called, would probably have been shared among three men.

3) The President would have a source of election outside the legislature. To no problem of the executive did the framers devote more time, talk, and votes. Most of the delegates originally shared Sherman's view that the executive "ought to be appointed by and accountable to the legislature only, which was the depository of the supreme will of the Society." Both the Virginia and the New Jersey plans provided for election of the executive by the legislature, and five times in the course of the Convention the delegates voted for this method. Not until the very end were enough of them swayed by the eloquence and diplomacy of Morris to adopt the electoral system outlined in Article II, Section 1, which was borrowed from the method for electing state senators in the Maryland Constitution of 1776. Morris and Wilson, an ill-assorted pair of prophets, were the only delegates to raise their voices clearly for election by the people. Another forty to fifty years would pass before the onward sweep of American democracy would carry the election of the President the rest of the way to the people, but the key decision in behalf of his independence was taken at Philadelphia: the removal of the machinery for choosing him to a location outside the legislature and beyond its control. The imagination goes limp before the thought of what the Presidency would be today if the framers had listened to Roger Sherman or George Mason.

4) The President would have a fixed term of office, which could be terminated only by the extraordinary method of conviction on impeachment for a high crime or misdemeanor. Hamilton devoted an entire number of *The Federalist* to

arguing the vast merits of this decision, which, he insisted, would guarantee the "personal firmness" of the President and the "stability" of his administration. Yet neither he nor any of his associates recognized the real implication of the fixed term: that it would render impossible the rise of a parliamentary form of government. They can hardly be blamed for not recognizing it, since the sharpest minds in England had not yet noticed how far their constitution had moved in the direction of responsible cabinet government.

5) The President would be eligible for re-election to an indefinite number of terms. Had this decision been taken differently, had no President been permitted even to seek a second term, the office would surely be a less splendid and powerful one than it is today. The second terms of Washington, Jackson, Wilson, the two Roosevelts, and Truman, landmarks in the evolution of the Presidency, would never have taken place at all; and their first terms, no mean landmarks themselves, would have been severely hampered had not friend and foe alike expected them to go for a second. And as Hamilton wrote in *The Federalist:*

> Would it promote the peace of the community, or the stability of the government to have half a dozen men who had had credit enough to be raised to the seat of the supreme magistracy, wandering among the people like discontented ghosts, and sighing for a place which they were destined never more to possess?

6) The President would be granted his own powers by the Constitution. It is a matter of great moment that he has prerogatives of his own, that all his authority does not come to him in the form of grants from Congress. What would he be without the constitutional right to command, nominate, pardon, negotiate treaties, supervise the execution of the laws, convene Congress, and, above all, defend himself with the qualified veto? How could Hamilton, writing as *Pacificus*, have vindicated Washington's proclamation of neutrality in 1793, how could the first Roosevelt have spun out his "Stewardship Theory," how could Chief Justice Taft have written the breath-taking opinion in *Myers* v. *U.S.*—if

the opening words of Article II were not so inclusive in their simplicity? "The executive power shall be vested in a President of the United States of America": could an apologist for the strong Presidency ask for anything more?

7) The President would not be encumbered with a council to which he would have to go for approval of his nominations or vetoes or other acts. In every state government of the time the executive was restrained in the use of one or more of his powers by a "council of revision," and the disappointed advocates of a plural executive insisted strenuously that the unity of the Presidency be qualified at least to this extent. "The Grand Signor himself," Mason grumbled, "had his Divan," but he grumbled in vain. The last of a persistent series of efforts to saddle the President with a council was beaten off at the end of the Convention. The unity of the executive had been preserved against all assaults.

8) A clause was inserted in Article I that would forbid any "person holding any office under the United States" to be a "member of either house during his continuance in office." The concern of the delegates over "corruption and the low arts of intrigue" was responsible for this copy of the ill-fated Place Bill of 1692; its real significance, which naturally escaped their notice, lay in the roadblock it still throws up against the evolution of any system of cabinet responsibility to Congress. A motion to strike this clause from the Constitution in preparation was frustrated by a tie vote. There is no telling what a President like James Monroe or Franklin Pierce might have made of the absence of this prohibition against a backstairs union of executive and legislature.

It is not hard to think of decisions the Convention might have taken to strengthen the Presidency even further. It could have fixed a longer term with indefinite re-eligibility, granted the President an item veto over appropriations, named four or five departments and made them clearly responsible to him, and required only a majority of the Senate for confirming treaties. But we can well be satisfied with Article II. When we realize that just two weeks from the end of the Convention the proposed Senate held exclusive authority to make treaties and appoint ambassadors and justices, we must marvel at the way in which the story came to a happy ending for Wilson and Morris.

The framers were fully aware, as they read over their finished work, that the Presidency would come under severe attack from those who had opposed the whole idea of the Convention from the beginning and were now about to learn that some of their worst fears had been realized. The case against the Presidency was well summed up in Patrick Henry's warning that this new executive office was an "awful squint toward monarchy." Hamilton, to be sure, proved equal to the task of refuting the charge. One can almost hear him sigh under the burden as he begins the eleven numbers of *The Federalist* devoted to the Presidency with the remark:

> There is hardly any part of the system which could have been attended with greater difficulty in the arrangement of it than this; and there is, perhaps, none which has been inveighed against with less candor or criticized with less judgment.

The big if silent gun in the arsenal of those who insisted upon the essential republicanism of the proposed Presidency was the universal assumption that George Washington, the Cincinnatus of the West, would be chosen as first occupant of the office—and chosen and chosen again until claimed by the grave. This assumption surely had something to do with the fact that all arguments over the executive at Philadelphia were resolved in favor of power and independence. As Pierce Butler wrote to a relative in England, "Entre nous, I do [not] believe they [the executive powers] would have been so great, had not many of the members cast their eyes toward General Washington as President; and shaped their ideas of the Powers to be given a President, by their opinions of his Virtue." And it made things a good deal easier for those who carried the brunt of the debate in 1788.

Let me now review briefly the outlines of the Presidency as it left the hands of the framers. Considering the temper of the times, it was an office of remarkable vigor and independence. Hamilton pointed out in *The Federalist* that it combined energy, unity, duration, competent powers, and "an adequate provision for its support" with "a due dependence on the people" and "a due responsibility." The President had a source of election divorced from the legislature, a fixed term, indefinite re-eligibility, immunity from conciliar advice that he had not sought, and broad constitutional powers of his own. It was his first task to run the government: to be its administrative chief, to appoint and supervise the bureaucrats, and to "take care that the laws be faithfully executed." He was to be ceremonial head of the nation, a republican king with the prerogative of mercy, and he was to lead the government in its foreign relations, whether peaceful or hostile. Despite the principle of the separation of powers, he was not to be completely isolated from the houses of Congress. To them he could tender occasional advice, and over their labors he held a qualified but effective veto. The President was to be a strong, dignified, nonpolitical chief of state and government. In a word, he was to be George Washington.

The Presidency today has the same general outlines as that of 1789, but the whole picture is a hundred times magnified. The President is all the things he was intended to be, and he is several other things as well. If we compare the Presidency under Washington with the Presidency under Eisenhower, we can see several remarkable changes in its character.

First, it is distinctly more powerful. It cuts deeply into the powers of Congress; in fact, it has quite reversed the expectations of the framers by becoming itself a vortex into which these powers have been drawn in massive amounts. It cuts deeply into the lives of the people; in fact, it commands authority over their comings and goings that Hamilton himself might tremble to behold.

Next, the President is more heavily involved in making national policy. It was, to be sure, the nineteenth-century Whigs who insisted most arrogantly that his sole task was to carry out the policies determined by an all-wise Congress, but even Washington cannot be said to have taken much of a hand in making policy except in the fields of foreign and military relations. Although Hamilton, his Secretary of the Treasury, exercised imaginative leadership and independent judgment in the areas he occupied by right or had invaded by stealth, his was considered at the time a virtuoso performance that would not be repeated. Yet it has been repeated and much improved upon by every President worth his salt. Whether as legislator, opinion-maker, commander, or administrator, the President molds lasting policy in every sector of American life.

To a large extent this is true because he is now so highly political a figure, and over this development the framers would have shaken their heads in wonder and sorrow. The plunge of the Presidency into party politics, which Jefferson took for himself and all his successors, may seem to us to have been unavoidable. The framers, however, would not have seen it that way. They believed sincerely in the idea of a patriot President, one who would rise coolly above the "heats of faction"; they would have considered it a mockery of all their pains to create a republican king if the king, like George III, were to turn his energies to party intrigue.

Another development would probably have shocked the framers, although one or two of them seem to have suspected that it was in the offing: the conversion of the Presidency into a democratic office. The extent to which he has become the "tribune of the people" is never so apparent as in an election year. When we contrast the decentralized, nonpolitical, dignified election of Washington with the "heats and ferments" of the presidential canvass as it has existed at least since 1840, we begin to sense how far the American people have gone to make this office their peculiar possession.

Finally, the office has a kind of prestige that it did not know under Washington and lacked as late as the turn of this century. Washington, after all, lent his prestige to the office, but today quite the reverse process takes place when a man enters the Presidency. He becomes the great figure in our system because the office is the great institution. We forget too easily that Congress—with sometimes the House on top and at other times the Senate—was the focus of the people's interest in their government through most of the first century under the Constitution. The Presidency carried with it very little of the magic that is now so notable an element in its strength.

All this evidence leads me to assert that the outstanding feature of American constitutional development has been the growth of the power and prestige of the Presidency. This growth has not been steady, but subject to sharp ebbs as well as massive flows. Strong Presidents have been followed by weak ones; in the aftermath of every "dictator" Congress has exulted in the "restoration of the balance wisely ordained by the fathers." Yet the ebbs have been more apparent than real, and each new strong President has picked up where the last one left off. Lincoln took off from Jackson and Polk, not from Pierce and Buchanan. Franklin Roosevelt looked back to Wilson over the barely visible heads of the three Presidents who came between them. As to the fate of the Presidency under the assaults of Thaddeus Stevens, Ben Wade, Schuyler Colfax, and their friends and heirs, I call Henry Jones Ford to witness: "Although once executive power, in the hands of an accidental President, was bent and held down by the weight of a huge congressional majority, its springs were unbroken, and it sprang up unhurt when the abnormal pressure was removed." In the face of history, it seems hard to deny the inevitability of the upward course of the Presidency—discontinuous, to be sure, but also irreversible.

Why should the Presidency have proved so resilient and resolute? Why has it outstripped both Congress and Court in the long race for power and prestige? The answer lies in the whole history of the United States. Let me dwell for a few pages on the major forces in our history that have hastened the ascent of the Presidency.

The first of these is the rise of the "positive state," the big government that regulates, stimulates, and operates in every part of the American economy and society and, further, strikes "a respectable posture of defense" in a shrinking world. The growth of our industrial civilization has brought in its train a thousand problems of huge concern to the American people, and the people have turned again and again to beg their national government for help in solving them. Congress has responded, too eagerly for some Americans and too timidly for others, by passing laws that reach deeply into our lives and even more deeply into our pockets. To execute these laws, Congress has created more than two million federal jobs. The positive state, that is to say, is the administrative state, and although much of the administration operates by design or default outside the President's range of supervision, much operates in his name and under his final direction. Moreover, as I have noted before, no law of Congress, no tricky technique aimed at insuring independence for some new arm of the positive state, can ever rob him of the exclusive constitutional power to "take care that the laws be faithfully executed." The historic shift in the nature of our Constitution away from a catalogue of limitations and toward a grant of powers has singled out the President as its chief beneficiary. Our progress as an industrial people has elevated him to a position of administrative authority without precedent in all history. Indeed, his authority is so vast that he cannot begin to exert it.

No book on an American subject is thought complete these days without a few insightful words from Alexis de Tocqueville, so I call upon that prince of cultural anthropologists to point out the second development that has raised the Presidency so high. Seeking for those "accidental causes which may increase the influence of executive government," De Tocqueville commented:

It is chiefly in its foreign relations that the executive power of a nation finds occasion to exert its skill and its strength. If the existence of the Union were perpetually threatened, if its chief interests were in daily connection with those of other powerful nations, the executive government would assume an increased importance in proportion to the measures expected of it and to those which it would execute.

So long as America held relatively aloof from the world, Congress could pose as the dominant branch of our government. Our self-elevation to the status of a major power, however, upset the old balance of the nineteenth century completely and finally. Woodrow Wilson wrote in Theodore Roosevelt's last year in office:

> The President can never again be the mere domestic figure he has been throughout so large a part of our history. The nation has risen to the first rank in power and resources. The other nations of the world look askance upon her, half in envy, half in fear, and wonder with a deep anxiety what she will do with her vast strength. . . . Our President must always, henceforth, be one of the great powers of the world, whether he act greatly or wisely or not. . . . We can never hide our President again as a mere domestic officer. We can never again see him the mere executive he was in the thirties and forties. He must stand always at the front of our affairs, and the office will be as big and as influential as the man who occupies it.

Even more influential and bigger, one may say with assurance, for even a Harding or Pierce or a succession of Fillmores could not remove America from the top of the world and turn the Presidency back into a cipher, and even an army of Radical Republicans in Congress led by a healthy Thad Stevens would not be equal to the tasks of negotiation and force. Congress continues to take a major part in shaping foreign policy and overseeing foreign affairs, but it can no longer challenge seriously the leadership of the President. We may take it as an axiom of political science that the more deeply a nation becomes involved in the affairs of other nations, the more powerful becomes its executive branch. The authority of the President has been permanently inflated by our entrance into world politics and our decision to be armed against threats of aggression, and as the world grows smaller, he will grow bigger.

An associated cause of the growth of the Presidency is the shattering series of emergencies, both foreign and domestic, that have been our lot during the past century. Another axiom of political science would seem to be this: great emergencies in the life of a constitutional state bring an increase in executive power and prestige, always at least temporarily, more often than not permanently. As proof of this point, we need only think of the sudden expansion in power that the Presidency experienced under Lincoln as he faced the rebellion, under Wilson as he led us into a world war, or under Franklin Roosevelt as he called upon Congress to extend him "broad Executive power to wage a war" against depression. Each of these men left the Presidency a stronger instrument, an office with more customary and statutory powers, than it had been before the crisis. Nor should we forget lesser Presidents in lesser crises, for these men, too, left their mark on the office. When Hayes dispatched troops to restore peace in the railroad strike of 1877, when McKinley sent 5,000 soldiers and marines to China during the Boxer uprising, and when Harry Truman acted on a dozen occasions to save entire states from the ravages of storm or fire or flood, the Presidency moved to a higher level of authority and prestige—principally because the people had now been taught to expect more of it.

The long decline of Congress has contributed greatly to the rise of the Presidency. The framers, as I have explained, expected Congress to be the focus of our system of government. The President was granted several of his powers, not so much for the sake of efficiency, as to keep him from being drawn out of his orbit into that of the legislature, there to tag along weakly in the wake of this sovereign force. What the framers did not reckon with was the astounding growth of the republic, which has turned Congress into a cumbersome, overstaffed pair of assemblies that speak in a confusion of tongues. Congress is a mighty instrument of constitutional democracy, one of which Americans may well be proud. Yet it is an instrument that cannot, by reason of its structure, constituency, and mission, do some things very well and other things at all. It cannot operate in the grand style without external leadership, which the President alone is in a position to offer. When Congress finally gave up primary responsibility for preparing the budget in 1921, it had no choice but to call on the President to come to the rescue. By abdicating an ancient function it could no longer perform, it gave a tremendous boost to the power of the President, not only to control his administration, but to influence the legislative process.

The knife of reality cuts even deeper: Congress generally cannot exercise its own authority without, in turn, increasing that of the President. There are obvious limits to what it can accomplish effectively by setting up independent commissions to execute new laws, and he must therefore be the chief beneficiary of most expeditions into unexplored territory. A delicious example of the way in which Congress is forced to expand his power while expanding its own is Title II of the Taft-Hartley Act of 1947. Few Congresses have ever distrusted presidential power more earnestly than that led by Joseph W. Martin and Robert A. Taft. Yet in enacting the long-awaited law "to bring the unions into line," it had to grant the President new statutory authority to act in major strikes. To make the whole episode even more delicious, it will be recalled that Mr. Truman spurned the gift, had it forced upon him by two-thirds of each house, and then used it spectacularly on ten separate occasions. Whether because of its exertions or insufficiencies, Congress has done its part to make the President what he is today.

Henry Jones Ford, in his perceptive *Rise and Growth of American Politics* (1898), was the first to call attention pointedly to the one giant force that has done most to elevate the Presidency to power and glory: the rise of American democracy. Most men who feared the proposed Presidency in 1787 were prisoners of the inherited Whig assumption that legislative power was essentially popular and executive power essentially monarchial in nature. The notion that a democratic President might be pitted against an oligarchical legislature occurred to few at the time—most notably to Gouverneur Morris, who spoke of the executive, with his tongue somewhere in his cheek, as "the guardian of the people" against the tyranny of the "great and wealthy who in the course of things will necessarily compose the Legislative body." As a matter of history, it took only about forty years to make Morris's masked prophecy come true. Since the days of Andrew Jackson the Presidency has been generally recognized as a highly democratic office. It depends directly on the people for much of its power and prestige; it shrinks to a rather mean thing when it loses their support. It is not, I feel sure, an accident of history that the upsurge of democracy and Jackson's resurrection of the Presidency went hand in hand, nor that he gave his name to the massive movement that swept him into office and bade him act boldly in the name of the people. Our Presidents could never have challenged Congress so often and successfully were they, too, not popularly elected and popularly sustained. American democracy finds in the President its single most useful instrument. Small wonder, then, that he stands as high as he does in the mythology and expectations of the American people. There is virtually no limit to what the President can do if he does it for democratic ends and through democratic means.

It is all very well to write about the forces that have made the Presidency what it is today, but I think it high time that I also wrote about men. None of these mighty events—the upbuilding of the positive state, our plunge into the world, the crises of war and depression, the hard times of Congress, or the triumph of democracy—would have had such influence on the Presidency if strong, alert, capable men had not come to this high office and shaped the event to their ends. The President acts every day, consciously or unconsciously, in the image of the Presidents who have gone before him. There are a hundred things he could not do, certainly not without raising a deafening outcry, if his predecessors had not done them already. The Presidents, too, helped build the Presidency, and I would therefore think it proper to devote the rest of this chapter to a review of the major contributions of the major Presidents. Just who those Presidents were—I count seven—will shortly become clear. At the same time, I shall not neglect entirely those other Presidents—I count six—who also gave strength to the Presidency, if only by defending it valiantly in a period of congressional ascendancy.

Let it be clear that I am judging these men as Presidents and weighing their contributions to the Presidency. Herbert Hoover is a much abler man than he was a President; James Madison's total impact on history should not be judged by his bumbling activities between 1809 and 1817.

George Washington enjoyed a long head start toward being a great President simply because he was the first President. This, however, is far from the whole story of George Washington. If he had not been willing to serve, another man— Adams or Rutledge or Jay or Clinton—would have been the first President, and the end of the affair might have been something quite different. We could call the roll of all those who ever held office anywhere in the United States and not come up with a single man who could have done the job that had to be done one-quarter as well as Washington. It was no easy trick to be the first occupant of a mistrusted office under a dubious Constitution. Two or three missteps might have touched off an irresistible demand for a new convention to undo the damage of Article II. But Washington, who had a nice feeling for the delicacy of his task, never did commit a serious misstep. His conduct was always eminently constitutional, and this, I think, was his most notable contribution to the Presidency. He proved the point that Hamilton had labored in *The Federalist:* that executive power was wholly "consistent with the genius of republican government" and even essential to the steady conduct of such government. "For he was no monarchist from preference of his judgment," Jefferson wrote some years after Washington's death. "The soundness of that gave him correct views of the rights of man, and his severe justice devoted him to them." Washington's Presidency was nothing if not painfully constitutional; he did the new republic and its chief office a mighty service in proving that power can ennoble as well as corrupt.

He did more than this, of course, for he lent his vast prestige to the republic and to the Presidency and thus rendered them acceptable to the American people. The Republicans in opposition may have ridiculed the pompous ceremonies in which the General thought it necessary to indulge, but they did not understand as clearly as he that magic may be reduced but never eliminated entirely from the processes by which free men are governed. Even they could not deny that his grand tours through the states strengthened the people's trust in the Constitution and excited their interest in the Presidency. Nor could they deny, indeed they were loud to lament, that he used his powers vigorously. Washington took time to make up his mind; he knew that any one of his decisions might set a precedent for generations to come. When he was ready to act, he acted with force and courage. The remarkable thing is how consistently he chose to act strongly rather than to abstain huffily, to advance rather than to retreat in his skirmishes with Congress over the uncharted territory left between them by the Constitution. In the field of foreign relations alone he set a dozen precedents that no later period of congressional ascendancy could ever erase—for example, the recognition of republican France, the proclamation of neutrality, the reception and dismissal of the French minister Genêt, the negotiation of Jay's Treaty, the use of executive agents, and the refusal to lay diplomatic correspondence before the House. Thanks to Hamilton he was an influential leader of legislation, thanks to his experience he was an excellent administrator, and thanks to himself he was a head of state who made every king alive seem like a silly goose. He was, in short, the best of all possible first Presidents. Constitutionalism, dignity, authority—these were his gifts to the Presidency and to the republic, and the greatest of these was constitutionalism. He never broke faith with the solemn truth he had proclaimed in his first inaugural address:

The preservation of the sacred fire of liberty and the destiny of the republican model of government are justly considered, perhaps, as *deeply*, as *finally*, staked on the experiment intrusted to the hands of the American people.

Lest we forget that Washington was also a human being, I insert this passage from Senator William Maclay's delightful

Journal, which describes a scene in which members of Congress waited upon the President:

> The President took his reply out of his coat pocket. He had his spectacles in his jacket pocket, having his hat in his left hand and his paper in his right. He had too many objects for his hands. He shifted his hat between his forearm and the left side of his breast. But taking his spectacles from the case embarrassed him. He got rid of this small distress by laying the spectacle case on the chimney piece. . . . Having adjusted his spectacles, which was not very easy considering the engagements of his hands, he read the reply with tolerable exactness and without much emotion.

The Presidency of Thomas Jefferson presents a slippery problem to the judgment of history. That he was a great man there can be no doubt, but that he was a great President there is considerable doubt. To his lasting credit are his injection of large doses of republicanism into an office that was coming to look just a shade too kingly, the breath-taking assertion of power (which took even his own breath away) in the purchase of Louisiana, and the flat declaration of presidential independence in his rejection of Marshall's subpoena in the Burr trial.

His most important contributions, of course, were his conversion of the Presidency to a political office and his leadership of Congress, and it is exactly at these two points that we run into trouble with Jefferson. His successes in molding and leading a party and then in using it to influence Congress leave us no choice but to judge him an effective President. Yet the very methods through which he brought strength to his own Presidency were calculated to weaken the office grievously once he had turned it over to lesser men, to men who were not and could never be the party chieftain that he was. John Marshall made a remarkable prediction about Jefferson's methods and influence in a letter written to Hamilton while the election of 1800 hung in the balance.

> Mr. Jefferson appears to me to be a man, who will embody himself with the House of Representatives. By weakening the office of President he will increase his personal power. He will diminish his responsibility, sap the fundamental principles of the government, and become

the leader of that party which is about to constitute the majority of the legislature.

We need not subscribe to the full bitterness of this statement to recognize that Marshall was a shrewd prophet. Jefferson did embody himself in the House of Representatives, thereby increasing his power ten times over. The power, however, was personal and not presidential. It flowed from him and not from his office. The leaders of Congress were his trusty lieutenants, the party caucus was his instrument to use pretty much as he pleased—so long as he did not wander from Republican principles. And who, after all, had first defined these principles? Timothy Pickering, another bitter foe, wrote that Jefferson tried to "screen himself from all responsibility by calling on Congress for advice and direction. . . . Yet with affected modesty and deference he secretly dictates every measure which is seriously proposed." This, I think, was the essence of Jefferson's Presidency. If we concentrate our gaze on his eight years, then shift it swiftly down to the middle of either the nineteenth or twentieth centuries, we can say that it was a strong and great Presidency. If we let our gaze halt at any year between 1809 and 1829, we must judge that Jefferson damaged the office severely by compromising its independence.

Andrew Jackson plucked Jefferson's chestnuts from the fire, although he would hardly have put it that way. Coming as it did after twenty years of congressional supremacy and government by commission, his resolute Presidency was, in Professor Corwin's words, "no mere revival of the office— it was a remaking of it." Jackson regained control over his own house by putting each department head in his place and cutting the Cabinet down to size, revived the veto and purified it on the niceties that had grown up around it, acted simultaneously as an imposing Chief of State and a hard-driving Chief of Party, and made clear to South Carolina that his power to execute the laws would be equal to the task of preserving the Union. He never missed an opportunity, by word or deed, to reassert the independence of an office that had become much more dependent on Congress than the framers could possibly have willed. His veto of the Bank Bill, his proclamation against the Nullifiers, and his "solemn protest" against the Senate's resolution of censure are assertions of presidential independence and authority that make exciting reading even today. Small wonder that Jackson's enemies, who remembered the years of Madison and Monroe, should judge his performance to be subversive of the republic. "I look upon Jackson," Chancellor Kent wrote to Justice Story, "as a detestable, ignorant, reckless, vain and malignant tyrant." "The President carries on the government," Webster cried in the Senate; "all the rest are subcontractors." And Clay spoke for all the Whigs:

> We are in the midst of a revolution, hitherto bloodless, but tending rapidly toward a total change of the pure republican character of the Government, and to the concentration of all power in the hands of one man.

Clay was right: he and his friends were caught in a revolution, but he was incapable of noting its origin or character. The revolution was abroad among the people, shifting the basis of our government from aristocracy to democracy without destroying its essential republicanism. Jackson was more a beneficiary than a leader of this revolution. He rode into office on a wave of protest that he never directed and barely understood himself. Yet he was exactly the kind of President—truculent, political, and demagogic—that the revolution needed to bring it full circle. The Presidency would surely have become a democratic office had Jackson never held it, but he was the one—we must give him respectful credit for it—who presided imperiously over the radical reversal in the roles of President and Congress as instruments of popular power and targets of popular feeling. And it is here, of course, that Clay and his friends went astray, for they could not rid their minds of the assumption—the very marrow of Whiggery—that executive power is inherently antipopular. Jackson's insistence that he, too, represented the people, at least as well as the House and better than the Senate, seemed to them the babbling of a fool or the bluster of a tyrant. No small part of his success may be traced directly to the fact that he was the first President of the United States elected by the people, and to the added fact that he knew it:

> The President is the direct representative of the American people; he possesses original executive powers, and absorbs in himself all executive functions and responsibilities; and it is his especial duty to protect the liberties and rights of the people and the integrity of the Constitution against the Senate, or the House of Representatives, or both together.

Jackson's mistakes were many, his legacies not all bright; more than one such President a century would be hard to take. Yet he was a giant in his influence on our system of government, and the influence, on balance, seems to have been wholesome. Well might he write in defense of his conduct: "I shall anticipate with pleasure the place to be assigned me in the history of my country."

The reaction to Jackson's Presidency was pronounced and prolonged; it was still in progress when Lincoln entered the White House. Yet the reaction, even though aided immeasurably by the depressing influence of the slavery issue on the Presidency, could never undo the work the old hero had done. The Jacksonian theory of the office prevailed, and Lincoln drew upon it in his hour of need.

Lincoln came to the Presidency with virtually no preparation and no preconception of the authority it embodied. But he had sworn "an oath registered in Heaven" to defend the Constitution, and in his inaugural address he promised his fellow citizens to save the Union without which the Constitution would be nothing but a scrap of paper. In sharp contrast to the vacillating Buchanan, who had denied his own authority to coerce a state to remain in the Union, Lincoln was ready to use military force to prevent secession. He had little concern for the form his actions might take; he meant only to act—as commander of the armed forces,

executor of the laws, and sole possessor of the shapeless grant
of power in the opening words of Article II.

It became necessary for me to choose whether, using only the existing
means, agencies, and processes which Congress had provided, I should
let the Government fall at once into ruin or whether, availing myself
of the broader powers conferred by the Constitution in cases of in-
surrection, I would make an effort to save it, with all its blessings,
for the present age and for posterity.

In his effort to save the government and the Union, Lincoln
pushed the powers of the Presidency to a new plateau high
above any conception of executive authority hitherto
imagined in this country. In the course of his famed eleven-
weeks' "dictatorship" he called out the militia, clamped a
blockade on the South, enlarged the regular army and navy
beyond their statutory limits, advanced public moneys to
persons unauthorized to receive them, pledged the credit
of the United States for a sizable loan, closed the mails to
"treasonable correspondence," authorized potential traitors
to be arrested, and suspended the writ of habeas corpus along
the line of communication between Washington and New
York. Most, but not all, of these actions were explained in
a message to Congress of July 4, the date he had selected
for convening the houses in special session.

These measures, whether strictly legal or not, were ventured upon
under what appeared to be a popular demand and a public necessity,
trusting then, as now, that Congress would readily ratify them. It is
believed that nothing has been done beyond the constitutional com-
petency of Congress.

And for the remainder of the war, as history records grate-
fully, he continued on his power-directed course, all but
oblivious of Congress, taking one extraordinary action after
another on the basis of the "war power." "As Commander-in-
Chief in time of war," he told some visitors from Chicago, "I
suppose I have a right to take any measure which may best
subdue the enemy." We need not look beyond the Emancipa-
tion Proclamation and the declaration of martial law in In-
diana to learn what he meant by "any measure."

There is a good deal more than this to tell about Lincoln's Presidency—the shabby performance as administrator, the creditable performance as diplomat, and the astounding performance as politician and leader of public opinion, not to mention the refusal of Congress to acquiesce in either the sweep or exclusiveness of his assertion of the war power. Enough has been said, I trust, to make this point clear: through the boldness of his untutored initiative, through an unprecedented plea of necessity, and through a unique interpretation of executive power, Lincoln raised the Presidency to a position of constitutional and moral ascendancy that left no doubt where the burden of crisis government in this country would thereafter rest. When Mr. Eisenhower's lieutenants speak of the "inherent powers of the Presidency" as our chief crutch in the wake of atomic disaster, they are reaching out to the mighty figure of Abraham Lincoln. And as they do, they should ponder the truth that Lincoln was a democrat as well as a "dictator," that he went to the well of power in behalf of humanity and rededicated the Presidency to the cause of liberty.

Lincoln, like Jefferson, left the Presidency temporarily enfeebled. The reaction was savage, and poor Andrew Johnson, a far braver President than Madison, was left to reap the wild wind that Lincoln had sowed unconcernedly when he permitted the War Department and Congress's Committee on the Conduct of the War to strike up an intimate relationship. There were times in the next thirty years—under Grant and Arthur and Harrison—when the Presidency seemed to have declined permanently in relation to Congress. But our rise to industrial might and our grand entrance upon the stage of world politics turned the course of the Presidency once more upward, and Colonel Roosevelt galloped into the White House as our first modern President.

It is hard to come to grips with Theodore Roosevelt, just as it is with any boy of six. There are times when he has the look of a genuinely great man, and times when he has the look, as Mark Hanna said, of a "damned cowboy." He was, beyond a doubt, a strong President, and no small part of his strength lay in the fact that he was a cowboy. For what Roosevelt gave the Presidency was the breathless drama of a Western movie, and he never left the audience in doubt that he was the "good guy" and the other fellows—Democrats, Senators, monopolists, Socialists, diplomats, nature fakers, muckrakers—the "bad guys." With the help of an attractive and active family, he put the Presidency on the front page of every newspaper in America, and there it has remained ever since with huge consequences for its status and authority. Teddy lived the dreams of every red-blooded American boy: he punched cattle, led a cavalry charge, became President, argued with the Pope, and, when it was all over, went off to shoot lions and elephants in Africa. Roosevelt himself describes a significant milestone in the evolution of the Presidency:

When the dinner was announced, the mayor led me in—or to speak more accurately, tucked me under one arm and lifted me partially off the ground, so that I felt as if I looked like one of those limp dolls with dangling legs carried around by small children. . . . As soon as we got in the banquet hall and sat at the head of the table the mayor hammered lustily with the handle of his knife and announced, "Waiter, bring on the feed!" Then, in a spirit of pure kindliness he added, "Waiter, pull up the curtains and let the people see the President eat."

T.R. contributed a great deal more to the office than a cheerful willingness to let the people see him eat. He was a brilliant molder and interpreter of public opinion, who confessed happily that the White House was a "bully pulpit." He scored several genuine triumphs as leader of Congress and thus gave substance to his theory that "a good executive under present conditions of American life must take a very active interest in getting the right kind of legislation." He conducted our diplomacy with unusual vigor, although his stick was not so big nor his voice so soft as he liked to boast. Still, the Panama Canal and the Treaty of Portsmouth were rather substantial achievements for those days, and who can say that he did not act grandly when he started the fleet off around the world and left it up to Congress to buy enough coal to bring it back?

Unfortunately for Teddy, but probably fortunately for the country, there was no real crisis in all his seven years that would permit him to prove conclusively that he was, as he insisted, a "Jackson-Lincoln" as opposed to a "Buchanan" President. The nearest thing to such a crisis was the anthracite coal strike of 1902, which he managed to settle before being pushed into executing his plans, first revealed fully in his *Autobiography* (1913), to have the army seize and operate the mines. This event, his land-withdrawals, and several other minor exertions of authority led him to state the famed "Stewardship Theory," which is still the most adroit literary justification of the strenuous Presidency:

> The most important factor in getting the right spirit in my Administration, next to the insistence upon courage, honesty, and a genuine democracy of desire to serve the plain people, was my insistence upon the theory that the executive power was limited only by specific restrictions and prohibitions appearing in the Constitution or imposed by the Congress under its Constitutional powers. My view was that every executive officer, and above all every executive officer in high position, was a steward of the people bound actively and affirmatively to do all he could for the people, and not to content himself with the negative merit of keeping his talents undamaged in a napkin. I declined to adopt the view that what was imperatively necessary for the Nation could not be done by the President unless he could find some specific authorization to do it. My belief was that it was not only his right but his duty to do anything that the needs of the Nation demanded unless such action was forbidden by the Constitution or the laws.

William Howard Taft, speaking also as an ex-President, derided the notion that the "executive . . . is to play the part of a universal providence and set all things right," and the strict theory of the Constitution is certainly with him. Whatever the theory, the facts have always been with Roosevelt in moments of extreme national emergency.

Woodrow Wilson was the best prepared President, intellectually and morally, ever to come to the White House. I have quoted several times from the chapter on the Presidency in his *Constitutional Government* (1908), and I think it fair to sum up the first four years of his Presidency by saying that he went as far as any man could go in converting those elegant, somewhat exaggerated words into reality. He was an able administrator, a shrewd leader of his party, a sensitive "spokesman for the real purpose and sentiment of the country," an impressive head of state, and, thanks to his academic theory of the President as a prime minister in relation to Congress, a genuinely effective leader of legislation. A devoted traditionalist, he was nevertheless unafraid of innovation. I would give a considerable sum to see a picture of Teddy Roosevelt's face when he picked up his evening paper April 8, 1913, and read that Wilson, honoring tradition and working innovation in the same act, had brought off successfully the first personal appearance of a President before Congress since the days of John Adams. Many historians think that the American Presidency, and with it our whole system of government, reached its highest peak of democracy, efficiency, and morality in the first four years of Woodrow Wilson.

In his second term, to be sure, he came to grief in more ways than one, although his record as a wartime President is every bit as admirable as the records of both Lincoln and the second Roosevelt. The most striking feature of this record is the way in which he acquired his vast authority over the American economy. Most of his emergency powers were delegated to him by laws of Congress. Confronted by the problem of raising and equipping an army to fight overseas rather than by a sudden threat to the republic, Wilson chose to demand express legislative authority for almost every unusual step. Lincoln had shown what the office was equal to in crises calling for solitary executive action. Now Wilson showed what it could do by working with the legislature. The source of Lincoln's power was the Constitution, and he operated in spite of Congress. The source of Wilson's power, except in the area of command and a few related matters, was a batch of statutes, and he co-operated with Congress.

In the end, sad to relate, he lost his hold on Congress, the country, and even himself. His appeal for a Democratic Congress in 1918 was a serious blunder; his whole course of action in behalf of the League of Nations foundered on his own obstinacy. Yet his journey to Europe in December 1918 was a herald of things to come, a rehearsal of the grand role the President would fill in the aftermath of World War II. Wilson carried the Presidency to new moral and political heights, and the strength of his days can be measured in the weakness of those that followed.

My seventh and last candidate for presidential greatness is Franklin D. Roosevelt, but I am going to put off the pleasure of dealing with him until Chapter 5. In the meantime, what of those men who, if not worthy to be ranked with Washington and Lincoln at the top, with Jackson and Wilson at the next level down, or with T.R. and Jefferson just below them, were none the less Presidents who turned in creditable performances? Let me call off these six names, several of which might not be on every historian's roll of strong but not quite great Presidents: James K. Polk, the one bright spot in the dull void between Jackson and Lincoln; Andrew Johnson, a man of few talents but much courage, whose protests against the ravages of the Radicals in Congress were a high rather than a low point in the progress of the Presidency; Rutherford B. Hayes, a vastly underrated President, whose successful struggle to name his own Cabinet, dogged devotion to civil service reform, seven stout vetoes of legislative riders, and dispatch of troops in the railroad strike of 1877 were all long steps forward from the Waste Land of Grant; Grover Cleveland, whose repeated displays of integrity and independence brought him very close to greatness in the Presidency; and Harry S. Truman and Dwight D. Eisenhower, of whom more hereafter.

This is not, be it noted, a list based chiefly on intelligence or even competence. There have been at least nine men—the two Adamses, Madison, Van Buren, Tyler, Arthur, McKinley, Taft, and Hoover—who were far better Presidents than Johnson from a technical point of view. None of them, however, was so important to the history of the Presidency as the despised man from Tennessee. To round out the presidential list, an irresponsible sort of exercise when done so abruptly, let me place Monroe, Fillmore, Benjamin Harrison, and Coolidge in the next slot down; W. H. Harrison, Taylor, and Garfield in a category that reads "insufficient data for ranking"; and Pierce, Buchanan, Grant, and Harding at the bottom. Buchanan was a man of rich experience, Grant a genuinely great general, and Harding a gentle man, but each in his own way was a near disaster for the Presidency. As for Pierce, let the gentle poet from New Hampshire have the last word:

> She had one President (pronounce him Purse,
> And make the most of it for better or worse.
> He's your one chance to score against the state).

It would be a near disaster for me to end this chapter on so low a note, and I therefore call attention once again to the six—I am still avoiding Mr. Roosevelt—who contributed most handsomely to the Presidency as it stands today. These men were more than eminent characters and strong Presidents. They were, or rather are, luminous symbols in our history. We, too, the enlightened Americans, feel the need of myth and mystery in national life—of magic parchments like the Declaration of Independence, of shrines like Plymouth and the Alamo, of slogans like "Fifty-Four Forty or Fight!", of hymns like "America," of heroics like Pickett's charge, of heroes like John Paul Jones. No one can have lived through Davy Crockett and deny the force of the American myth; no one can stand at Gettysburg and deny its meaning. And who fashioned the myth? Who are the most satisfying of our folk heroes? With whom is associated a wonderful web of slogans and shrines and heroics? The answer, plainly, is the six Presidents I have pointed to most proudly. Each is an authentic folk hero, each a symbol of some virtue or dream especially dear to Americans. Together they make up almost half of the company of American giants, for who except Christopher Columbus, Benjamin Franklin, Daniel Boone, Robert E. Lee, and Thomas A. Edison in real life, Deerslayer and Ragged Dick in fiction, and Paul Bunyan and the Lonesome Cowboy in myth can challenge them for immortality? Washington the spotless patriot, Jefferson the democrat, Jackson the man of the frontier, Lincoln the emancipator and preserver of the Union, Theodore Roosevelt the All-American Boy, Wilson the peacemaker—these men are symbols of huge interest and value to the American people.

Lincoln is the supreme myth, the richest symbol in the American experience. He is, as someone has remarked neither irreverently nor sacrilegiously, the martyred Christ of democracy's passion play. And who, then, can measure the strength that is given to the President because he holds Lincoln's office, lives in Lincoln's house, and walks in Lincoln's way? The final greatness of the Presidency lies in the truth that it is not just an office of incredible power but a breeding ground of indestructible myth.

CHAPTER **4**

THE MODERN PRESIDENCY

☆

The Presidency to which Dwight D. Eisenhower came on January 20, 1953 was a visibly different office from the Presidency that Herbert Hoover had surrendered on March 4, 1933. In the course of these twenty years it had been laden with all kinds of new duties by a people unwilling to submit patiently to the disorders of an industrial civilization or to withdraw sullenly from the turmoils of a mad world. It had taken on all kinds of new help, both personal and institutional, to save it from collapse under the mounting burdens of war and peace. And it had moved even higher, if that were possible, in the esteem of the American people, most of whom counted it a mighty weapon in the struggle for liberty and security at home and abroad. The Presidency had been modernized—conspicuously if not completely.

My purpose in this chapter is to examine the new dimensions added to the office by Presidents Roosevelt and Truman. Lest it be thought that this is a partisan review, I hasten to point out that our Republican President has moved ahead, steadily if not quite so theatrically, with the work of modernization begun by the Democrats who preceded him. If he is not as strong a President as Roosevelt or Truman, he occupies an equally strong Presidency. He is, in any case, the first beneficiary of two decades of unusual executive activity. The Presidency, like any vital institution, is always in transition, but this has been an especially propitious period for change and growth. I turn therefore to an analysis

of the most notable departures in the authority and structure of the Presidency in the past quarter-century.

The first change is in the working relations of President
and Congress. I have already made some comments on the
President's part in the lawmaking process, the sum of which
was that he has now become a sort of prime minister or "third
House of Congress." He is no longer restricted in his legislative activities to the points of input and output on the
congressional transmission belt, that is, to recommending
measures in general terms at one end and then, after sitting
quietly for a decent or indecent interval, to stamping the
mangled results "OK" or "Reject." Rather, he is now expected to make detailed recommendations in the form of
messages and proposed bills, to watch them closely in their
tortuous progress on the floor and in committee in each
house, and to use every honorable means within his power
to persuade the gentlemen of Congress to give him what he
wanted in the first place. One of the chief concerns of the
modern President is to push politely but relentlessly for
enactment of his own or his party's legislative program. If
he lacks a program of the most detailed nature, he is considered a sluggard; if he cannot persuade Congress to enact
at least a few of the details, he is considered a failure. We
judge our Presidents today largely by their success in leading
Congress.

It was not always thus. The role of the President as active
participant in every stage of the legislative process is almost
wholly the creation of three twentieth-century incumbents—
Theodore Roosevelt, Woodrow Wilson, and Franklin D.
Roosevelt. Each of these men came to the Presidency from
a successful tenure as governor of a progressive state, and
the extent of his success had been measured in terms of his
leadership of the legislature. Each came at a time when the
state of the Union demanded that new laws be placed on the
books; none was strangled by wearing the "old school tie"
of either house of Congress. The meeting of their forceful
personalities with the crises of the age produced a revolution

in the relations of the President to Congress and in the standards by which the people judge his total performance.

This revolution, it should be noted, was still unfinished in the last days of Franklin Roosevelt, for Congress, the party of the second part, remained unconvinced of the President's right to interest himself so actively in its independent activities. The members of Congress could hardly be blamed for believing that the times were out of joint, that Roosevelt had exerted a kind of leadership that would not outlast his incumbency or the end of the emergency, and that there would be a retreat to Hoover—if never again to Harding—under the next President. But the next President, despite the perky pride with which he himself wore the old school tie, refused to play dead. Mr. Truman kept the pressure on throughout his eight years, even when his hopes of accomplishing anything constructive must have been entirely empty, and by the end of his second term even the Republicans in Congress were waiting politely for his proposals on labor, taxes, inflation, and education. What is still more revealing of the change of climate, they considered it a wholly natural thing to be invited to the White House to hear from the President directly what he had in mind. Things had moved a long way from the days when Senator George F. Hoar had testified:

The most eminent senators would have received as a personal affront a private message from the White House expressing a desire that they should adopt any course in the discharge of their legislative duties that they did not approve. If they visited the White House, it was to give, not to receive, advice. Any little company or coterie who had undertaken to arrange public policies with the president and to report to their associates what the president thought would have rapidly come to grief. . . . Each of these stars kept his own orbit and shone in his sphere, within which he tolerated no intrusion from the president or from anybody else.

This development has been carried the rest of the way—beyond the point of no return, I would judge—by President Eisenhower. That point was reached and passed in a press conference on January 13, 1954. During the first session of the Eighty-third Congress Mr. Eisenhower had submitted few proposals to Congress and had exerted little continuous pressure in their behalf. Observers were wondering aloud whether he was aware of the change that had come over the Presidency or of Congress's need for guidance. But as the second session approached the President began to gather steam, and within a few days of the opening of Congress in 1954 he was sending over detailed messages outlining his wishes on farm policy, social security, foreign policy, labor, and finance. And now at the press conference this exchange took place:

Q. Mr. President, could you say what percentage of your recommended proposals you would expect to be passed at this session?

A. The President said, Look, he wanted to make this clear. He was not making recommendations to pass the time away or to look good. . . . He was going to work for their enactment. Make no mistake about that. That was exactly what he was in the White House for and what he intended to do.

Twenty-five years ago this remark, especially as and to whom delivered, would have brought most members of Congress spluttering to their feet and set the President's few remaining friends to shaking their disbelieving heads. Even as late as ten years ago it would have been considered a gratuitous insult by the die-hards and a show of bad taste by the moderates in Congress. In 1954 it passed unchallenged and even unnoticed, except by those whose reaction was, "Well, it's about time."

Since that moment of awakening President Eisenhower has done his best to make good his pledge. He has used arts of persuasion that were once controversial but are now considered altogether regular, and that is the essence of this first ingredient of the modern Presidency: the irregular has become the regular, the unexpected the expected, in the area of executive-legislative relations. The President has no weapons that were not available to Harding or, for that matter, to McKinley. The appeal to the people is more easily brought off in the age of electronics; on the other hand, the dangled patronage has lost much of its influence thanks to the success of civil service reform. The White House conference, the appeal to party loyalty, the threat of a veto—these weapons, too, are no keener than they were a half-century ago. The President's own machinery for drafting legislative proposals and for maintaining good relations with Congress is vastly enlarged and improved, but the houses themselves, despite the pleas of Senators Kefauver and Monroney, have made no important institutional changes in recognition of his increased responsibility for providing them with leadership. And the Constitution, needless to say, reads exactly as it did 169 years ago in those passages that govern the relations of executive and legislature. The remarkable change in these relations has been neither institutional nor constitutional, but rather meteorological—a change in the climate of politics and custom. The country now expects the President to have a program and to work hard for its enactment. He is more likely to be criticized in today's press for timidity and inertia than for resolution and activity. What the country expects, Congress also expects. Henceforth it will react with irritation rather than indignation to presidential attempts to goad it into action.

The President's right, even duty, to propose detailed legislation to Congress touching every problem of American society, and then to speed its passage down the legislative transmission belt, is now an accepted usage of our constitutional system. So far has this revolution gone that the thought occurs: we need new standards with which to judge the "strength" of a President.

The rise of the President as active leader of Congress has been accompanied by a second change—the opening of new channels of communication through which he can mold, measure, and follow public opinion. Who can say how much power and drama have flowed toward the President and away from the houses of Congress because he can chat with the nation easily over radio and television and they cannot? "Capitol Cloakroom" and "Face the Nation" are hardly in the same class as a fifteen-minute broadcast and telecast from the White House. Nor can the "spectaculars" staged by Senators McCarthy and Kefauver for the housewives of America be said to have raised our interest in or respect for Congress as an institution. Let us acknowledge that the President has been the chief gainer from the miracles of electronics, and let us pray that Congress never succumbs to the urge to compete with him by putting its regular proceedings on the air. What Stephen Potter would call the "natural one-upness" of the President is a hard fact of life with which Congress must learn to live.

The most influential channel of public opinion to and from the President that has been opened up in recent years is the press conference. The President's regular meeting with the press is now a completely accepted institution, and it therefore comes as a surprise to recall that its unbroken existence in present form dates only from the first year of Franklin Roosevelt. The Presidents have been in close touch with the press from the beginning, but not until the administration of Woodrow Wilson was the regularly scheduled conference, open to newspapermen as a matter of right and not of personal privilege, established on a fixed footing. When America entered World War I, Wilson abandoned the conference to avoid embarrassment to his administration, and the three Republican Presidents who followed him were unable or unwilling to match his able performance between 1913 and 1917. Harding made such a mess of several hot grounders hit in his direction that he changed the rules and required questions to be written out and submitted in advance; Coolidge continued this practice and generally kept the press at arm's length; and Hoover, who also insisted on written questions, held fewer and fewer conferences until finally, as the darkness gathered, he abandoned them altogether.

Franklin Roosevelt, who would have been lost without the press, revived the conference and brought it to new heights of influence and public interest. Any journalist certified by the correspondents' own association was admitted to the conference, and questions were asked and answered "from horseback." Roosevelt maintained the wise rule first laid down by Wilson that he was not to be quoted directly without specific permission, but otherwise the conference became a wonderful game of give-and-take. Mr. Truman, despite some occasional lapses in his first term, carried forward the precedents set by President Roosevelt. He gets credit for shifting the conference from the President's office to the "treaty room" in the old State building, an auditorium with seats for several hundred persons, and thus for establishing it on a much more formal basis.

Mr. Eisenhower, too, has acted as if it were both "an Honor and a Privilege" to meet the press once a week when he is in Washington. On January 19, 1955, a day to remember, he presided over the first press conference ever to be filmed by television and newsreel cameras; millions of Americans sat at home that evening and watched their President go through his paces. He went through them, let it be recorded, with an air of dignity, sincerity, and competence, and even the most hardened observers fell all over themselves praising this "marvelous example of democracy at work." There were some complaints, largely political in inspiration, over the decision of the White House to review the footage before releasing it to the telecasters and movie companies, but this was a perfectly proper extension of the well-understood prohibition against quoting the President directly without permission. The experiment having succeeded, the televised press conference has become a regular weekly feature. As might be expected, it is losing its appeal to many people, and most networks now present only excerpts from the conference. The moral is an old one, familiar to all the able Presidents: when you find a bright new tool, don't dull it with too much use. So long as the televised press conference is not overdone, it bids well to remain an important, not to say informative and entertaining, technique of American democracy.

Televised or not, the presidential press conference is now a fixed custom in our system of government. It is conceivable that a President with no taste for this kind of half-circus, half-inquisition could cut the growth of custom short, but the next President would be certain—in fact, he would pledge himself bravely while still a candidate—to start it up again. In part this is true because the people have come to expect it and dislike being disappointed in their expectations, in part because it is, on balance, so useful a platform for the man who stands on it. No President can afford to be without it, certainly no sociable, outgoing President of the kind we are likely to elect from now on.

There has been considerable talk in the press and in textbooks about the kinship of the President's press conference and the question-and-answer period in the British House of Commons. The press conference does serve us in some ways as a method for interrogating the government of the hour, but several sharp differences are to be noted. The President controls the questions, if only by retreating into the shell of "no comment," as the Prime Minister does not. The questioners are in no sense his peers, even though they like to think of themselves as representatives of the American people, a fourth estate with a grave responsibility. And the questions must generally be of a kind that, far from nailing him to the wall on a specific point, permit him to take off on a free flight in any direction he chooses. The Prime Minister has not, to the best of my knowledge, been asked to enlighten the people of England on the origin, nature, or destiny of flying saucers, while President Eisenhower has already assured us that they do not come from outer space. The fact is that the President could not ask for a tool of leadership more perfectly designed to his ends, for a pulpit more artfully constructed from which to preach sermons to us and to the world, for a listening device more finely tuned to hear the legitimate complaints of the people. The press conference is not a restraining but an enabling device, as our last three Presidents have demonstrated repeatedly; and that, I would guess, is why it will never again be abandoned outright nor even reduced to the cold, gray event it was under Herbert Hoover. An unbriefed, irritable, shoot-from-the-hip sort of President may do himself serious damage in the give-and-take of the press conference, but so may he in reaching out along any of his channels to the people.

I conclude with a comment from Louis Brownlow, certainly the wisest head among those who watched the press conference grow to its present stature:

> It would be almost impossible, in my opinion, for any President now to change this pattern or to interfere in any material way with this institution, set up without authority of law, required by no Constitutional mandate, embodying no rights enforceable in a court of law, but nevertheless an institution of prime importance in the political life of the American people.

It would be almost impossible and altogether imbecile. No President in his right mind would surrender gladly the power he draws from this unique institution, which puts him, in a light that he selects for himself, on the front page of every newspaper in the land and, as often as not, in the world.

The role of the President that has undergone the most rapid growth in the past quarter-century is that of Protector of the Peace. Thanks to the eagerness with which Roosevelt and Truman responded to calls for help from the people, we now think of the President as a one-man riot squad ready to rush anywhere in the country to restore peace and order. While state and local authorities usually deal with fire, drought, flood, or violence, disasters that spread over several states or touch upon federal interests or are simply too hot for a locality to handle can be sure of attention and action from the White House.

This is especially true of labor disputes that disturb the peace of the United States. The sudden expansion of government interest in labor-management relations under the New and Fair Deals has worked visible influence upon the office and powers of the President. He has little to do with the normal processes of government participation in such relations, but in labor disputes that are national emergencies he has now become, even when he refuses to act, a dominant third party. The Taft-Hartley Act of 1947 speaks wistfully of "sound and stable industrial peace." The prime responsibility of the President to preserve and protect that peace is now universally assumed. His powers in this area fall under three headings:

1) The power literally to "keep the peace of the United States" by instituting military action in strikes attended by violence and public disorder.

In most cases the policing of disorderly strikes is the duty of state and local authorities. The President will intervene in industrial warfare in two situations only: when he has been requested to act by the proper authorities, who thereby acknowledge their own inability to preserve order; or when federal laws and rights are being openly flouted and the national interest in a restoration of order is clear. The President may refuse to intervene when asked; he may also, as Cleveland proved in the Pullman strike of 1894, intervene unbidden and even unwanted. In recent years this power has rested on the shelf. We seem to have less violence in our labor disputes, and local officials seem better qualified to handle them in the severe yet neutral fashion the public interest demands. Yet the power remains in the President's possession, stretching all the way from the mere threat of force to outright martial law, and I suspect we will live to see it used again.

2) The power to remove obstructions to the flow of industrial production in time of war, or just before or after war.

The President must display unusual interest in wartime labor disputes. As Commander in Chief he is concerned before all others that production and delivery of weapons and supplies continue without interruption. Under conditions of total war he becomes the dominant figure in industrial relations. His power is exerted along two related lines. First, he makes it his immediate business to see that peaceful relations are maintained between labor and management. To this end he institutes special agencies to aid them in resolving their differences. Second, he enforces the rulings and orders of these agencies by applying "indirect sanctions"—for example, by focusing publicity on a recalcitrant union or employer, by threatening to reclassify workers in the draft, or by cutting off a plant's supply of scarce raw materials—and he prevents critical work stoppages by the final sanction of presidential seizure. Presidents Roosevelt and Truman both wielded this vast authority with vigor and considerable success. Between them they ordered more than sixty seizures in the years 1941-1946. The most notable of these was the "Battle of Montgomery Ward," in which the enemy was defeated by the simple maneuver of having its commander, Mr. Sewell Avery, carried from his office by two bewildered enlisted men of the United States Army. This power received a salutary if hardly crippling check in the Steel Seizure case of June 1952.

3) The power to intervene in disputes that constitute economic national emergencies.

Quite apart from the open threat to our national well-being presented by large-scale violence or a halt in war production is the continuing problem of strikes in the basic industries and transportation system. The American people know from experience how injurious a widespread stoppage of work in the telephone system or steel mills can be, and long before Judge T. Alan Goldsborough began his famous lecture course for John L. Lewis, which the student failed miserably, we were aware that a strike of long duration in the railroads or coal mines might cause "society itself" to "disintegrate." It is therefore not surprising that the wave of strikes in 1946 and 1947 should have persuaded the authors of the Taft-Hartley Act to insert broad provisions authorizing the President to act in disputes "imperilling the national health and safety." He already had some power in this area—his prestige as President, which allowed him to intervene informally in the manner of Theodore Roosevelt in the anthracite coal strike of 1902, and a grant of limited authority, which had been enfeebled by overwork, in the Railway Labor Act of 1926. Now Congress was prepared to go further and empower the President to seek an injunction in the federal courts that would delay a crippling strike for eighty days.

Although Mr. Truman, in vetoing the Taft-Hartley Act, expressed particular disapproval of its emergency provisions, he made use of them on seven occasions in 1948 and on three in his second term, for the most part with circumspection and considerable success. Mr. Eisenhower, who presides in less turbulent times and is more reluctant than Mr. Truman to brandish this kind of power, has used them only once.

It should be plain to see that from this time forward the most important single factor in labor disputes "imperilling the national health and safety" will be the heart, mind, and politics of the President of the United States. And whatever statutory techniques of government intervention we possess at present or may develop in the future, his matchless capacity to mobilize and express public opinion will remain his keenest weapon. Any permanent solution to this problem that overlooks his role as Protector of the Peace is doomed to disorder and early sorrow.

The President's position in labor disputes is as delicate as his powers are vast. As final guardian of the public interest he must stand clear of partisanship and wield his weapons with discretion and economy. In particular, he must avoid using them in such a manner that one of the parties to a dispute will go out of its way to invite intervention. He must recognize that his powers in this field are emergency powers only, that the regular processes of collective bargaining and of government mediation and conciliation are not to be disturbed. He must resist the temptation to interpose his prestige in disputes that are being threshed out, however slowly, by regular statutory and administrative machinery—or he may pull down the whole structure of government intervention about his ears. "Equality for both and vigilance for the public welfare" must be the President's high resolve.

Vast though his powers are, we are better off with them than without them. It is reassuring to know that in an economic system that invites and rewards the struggle for self-interest there is a boundary beyond which the contestants will push at their peril—and that there is a high sheriff to patrol it.

It might be well to close this discussion by recalling my comments in Chapter 1 on a role that is still very much in its infancy, that of Manager of Prosperity. The President is now expected to act before and not just after an economic crisis develops, and he is steadily amassing powers with which to do it. It is still too early to measure the full dimensions of this role, but not too early to recognize that they are genuinely impressive. When we come face to face with the next great threat of depression, the President, whoever he may be, will be a "spectacle unto the world."

If there is any one point I have hammered at in this book, it is that the Presidency is an essentially democratic office. The people have done much to make it what it is today; the man who holds it reaches out to them for support and repays them with guidance and protection. There is no more impressive evidence of this truth than a fourth development in the modern Presidency: the elevation of this office to a commanding position in the ongoing struggle for civil liberties and civil rights. We have become increasingly conscious of our shortcomings and wrongdoings in these related fields in recent years. Even as we sin against one another in the area of freedom of expression, even as we drag our feet in the march toward justice for our minorities, we feel the gaze of the whole world upon our necks and are uncomfortable. And as we have become more conscious, the President, who has a sizable part of this world for a constituency, seems to have grown in stature as a friend of liberty.

Here as everywhere he operates under severe limitations. A wing of his party may have a stake in discrimination; public opinion may be riding a wave of intolerance; Congress may refuse him even the most watered-down authority to protect minorities against intimidation. Yet there are many things he can do if he is resolute and perceptive, if he steers a middle course between serene abstention and demagogic meddling in events and areas critical for American liberty. Here are some of his powers, all but one or two of them the creations of our last three Presidents:

He can recommend legislation to Congress—in the grand style of Harry S. Truman's message of February 2, 1948, which made ten controversial proposals ranging from the establishment of a Fair Employment Practices Commission to home rule for the District of Columbia, or in the more modest manner of Dwight D. Eisenhower's request for reconsideration of certain procedures established in the McCarran-Walter Act of 1952.

He can veto illiberal legislation, as Presidents Cleveland, Taft, and Wilson all vetoed bills that set up a literacy test for immigrants. (For the record, such a bill was finally passed into law over Wilson's veto in 1917.)

He can make broad use of his authority as Commander in Chief. Like Roosevelt he can establish an F.E.P.C. by executive order as a means of speeding up production in time of war, like Truman he can establish a President's Committee on Equality of Treatment and Opportunity in the Armed Forces, and like Eisenhower he can push ahead with the work begun by his two predecessors aimed at eliminating segregated units in all branches of the service.

He can issue similar orders and push for similar practices in his capacity as Chief Executive. Examples of this use of presidential authority are Truman's regulations of 1948 prohibiting discrimination in personnel practices "throughout the Federal establishment" and Eisenhower's Committee on Government Contracts, which was set up to secure compliance with fair employment practices by companies with government contracts.

He can use his power of appointment to strengthen the Supreme Court as a bulwark of freedom, or to bring acknowledged friends of civil liberty and representatives of minority groups into the top levels of the administration; he can use his power of removal, if he doesn't mind the storm he will surely raise, to dismiss officials who insist on ignoring or even sabotaging his antidiscrimination orders.

He can, like Mr. Eisenhower, order the Attorney General to file a brief as "friend of the court" in private suits against segregation in education; he can, like Mr. Truman, order the Attorney General to institute actions under Title 18, Chapter 13, Sections 241-242 of the *United States Code*. These provisions, which date from 1870, make it a federal offense to engage in various activities that "injure, oppress, threaten, or intimidate any citizen in the free exercise or enjoyment of any right or privilege secured to him by the Constitution or laws of the United States." They are not easy to use, but an occasional conviction has been obtained under them. The President can also prod the F.B.I. to be on the alert for offenses in this category.

He can establish commissions of distinguished citizens to survey and report on the state of freedom in this country. The leading example of such a commission was Mr. Truman's Committee on Civil Rights, which made a memorable report in 1947. And as Mr. Eisenhower has proved in his dealings with the Wright Commission, he may also co-operate with a group set up by Congress to survey and improve the rights of government employees.

He can use a number of his ancient and honorable powers to advance the cause of justice and humanity—for example, the pardoning power to correct a sentence made heavier because of the criminal's race, the treaty-making power to pledge his own faith (if not the Senate's) to wiping genocide from the face of the earth, and his power as chieftain of his party to bring leaders of minorities into its high councils.

He can take special pains to eliminate the disgraceful vestiges of discrimination in the District of Columbia. Although Mr. Truman was doubtless correct in denying that he had the power to end racial segregation outright in the District by executive order, there is much the President can do with a quiet order here and a good example there. For example, Attorney General Brownell's vigorous intervention in a case in 1953 resulted in the Supreme Court's upholding legislation prohibiting discrimination in Washington restaurants, after which a commissioner of the District government appointed by the President gave restaurant owners forty-eight hours to comply with the law.

Finally, and most important, he can use his authority as

spokesman for the nation in such a way as to inspire those who are working for a more democratic America and to rebuff those who would drag us backward into the swamps of primitivism and oppression. The moral force of this great office is never so apparent as when he lashes out at the vigilantes who terrorize librarians and school boards, at the little foxes who spoil the vines of democracy.

I am aware that I have given only one side of the picture in this review. The President also has it in his power to dampen the struggle for civil rights by his indifference and to invade the field of civil liberties in force. Franklin Roosevelt's order authorizing the evacuation of all persons of Japanese ancestry from the Pacific coast in early 1942 and the combined Truman-Eisenhower record in the area of loyalty and security are proof that even the most conscientious President may blunder or be pressured into dubious acts. I am aware, too, as I noted at the outset of this discussion, that he must use his powers shrewdly and with a feeling for limits. He cannot, for example, comment critically on every patent violation of liberty and justice throughout the land, especially when the violence is done by judges and juries. Yet he is now in a position to be one of the most potent forces behind our progress in civil rights and our defense of civil liberties. From this time forward the President will have no choice but to serve as the conscience and strong right arm of American democracy.

The most notable development in the Presidency in recent years is a change in structure rather than a growth in power, although the latter is certainly the first cause of the change. As the burdens of the President have mounted steadily, he has taken on auxiliary machinery to help him bear them. Inseparable from the modern Presidency, indeed essential to its effective operation, is a whole train of officers and offices that serve him as eyes, ears, arms, mouth, and brain. The encompassing title of this machinery is the Executive Office of the President, and it numbers roughly 1,200 persons whose sole purpose in public life is to help the President discharge his duties. The Executive Office exists for him, and he could not exist without it.

The Executive Office was established in 1939 through the associated, if not entirely harmonious, endeavors of Franklin D. Roosevelt and the Seventy-sixth Congress. The immediate impulse for organizing it was Roosevelt's own candid recognition that an otherwise professional performance during his first term in the Presidency had been hampered by the number of his duties and by the lack of assistance in their discharge. He was not the first person to make this discovery. Long before the New Deal began to pile new burdens on the Presidency, students of the national government, the most vocal of them the Presidents themselves, had been calling the attention of Congress and the nation to the hapless plight of the "final object of the public wishes."

Mr. Roosevelt's solution was thoroughly in character. Never one to let an important problem lie around unstudied by a special commission, he set the wheels turning in early 1936 with the appointment of the President's Committee on Administrative Management. Under the adroit guidance of Louis Brownlow (Chairman), Charles E. Merriam, and Luther Gulick, a corps of noted scholars probed every part of the federal administration. Particular attention was devoted to the heart of the system, the Presidency itself. The Committee reported to Mr. Roosevelt in January 1937, and in the shortest scholarly sentence on record told him what he had known ever since his first day in the White House: "The President needs help." In forwarding the Committee's reports to Congress, Mr. Roosevelt summed up the parlous state of the Presidency in these words:

The Committee has not spared me; they say, what has been common knowledge for twenty years, that the President cannot adequately handle his responsibilities; that he is overworked; that it is humanly impossible, under the system which we have, for him fully to carry out his constitutional duty as Chief Executive, because he is overwhelmed with minor details and needless contacts arising directly from the bad organization and equipment of the Government. I can testify to this. With my predecessors who have said the same thing over and over again, I plead guilty.

The controversial recommendations of the President's Committee ranged the whole field of executive management. Central to its purposes, however, was the immediate problem of the presidential burden, which it proposed to lighten by creating a team of six executive assistants and an administrative staff of experts who would handle the President's managerial functions in budgeting, planning, and personnel. These proposals ran afoul of the epic battle over the "Court-packing" scheme and the efforts of numerous members of the Seventy-fifth Congress to pin the label of "dictator" on the President. Not until two years later did Congress grudgingly bestow on Mr. Roosevelt a limited power of executive reorganization. The sweeping proposal of the Committee on Administrative Management that "the whole Executive Branch of the Government should be overhauled and the present 100 agencies reorganized under a few large departments in which every executive authority would find its place" was frustrated by those sections of the Reorganization Act that forbade the President to lay profane hands upon a full nineteen agencies, including the Civil Service Commission. With the latter exception, however, he was able to deal pretty much as he saw fit with his own problems.

This he did in Executive Order 8248, dated September 8, 1939, and described correctly by Mr. Gulick as a "nearly unnoticed but none the less epoch-making event in the history of American institutions." The effect of the order was to create the Executive Office, designate six components within it, and authorize the President to appoint the personal assistants for whom the Committee on Administrative Management had called. The logic of this order can be most clearly grasped by quoting a passage from Professor Leonard D. White, in which he has succeeded admirably in expressing the "basic objectives" underlying the "proper organization of any large-scale executive office in government." These, it would seem, were the purposes for which the Executive Office was created:

1. To insure that the chief executive is adequately and currently informed.

2. To assist him in foreseeing problems and planning future programs.

3. To ensure that matters for his decision reach his desk promptly, in condition to be settled intelligently and without delay; and to protect him against hasty and ill-considered judgments.

4. To exclude every matter that can be settled elsewhere in the system.

5. To protect his time.

6. To secure means of ensuring compliance by subordinates with established policy and executive direction.

There was a more profound purpose, too, for this was a President, not just a department head, who was to be rescued from paralyzing detail—but more of that presently.

Through all the years of crisis since 1939 the Executive Office has functioned at a high level of proficiency and morale. By no means a faultless instrument of public administration, it has nevertheless served President and nation with distinction and has given an entirely new cast to the question of executive management in the national government, as well as to the Presidency itself. For some years now it has been popular, even among his friends, to write off Mr. Roosevelt as a "second-rate administrator." In the light of Executive Order 8248, an accomplishment in public administration superior to that of any other President, this familiar judgment seems a trifle musty.

Rather than wander wearily through the many changes in the Executive Office under each of the last three Presidents, let me describe the major components that exist today, and let me name enough names to express the very personal flavor that characterizes their operation. This is the President's "general staff":

The White House Office, which serves him directly and intimately, numbers about a dozen top-flight personal aides, two dozen aides to these aides, and roughly 325 clerks, stenographers, messengers, and secretaries who are needed to handle the documents and correspondence that descend upon the White House in torrents. Among those who are nearest to Mr. Eisenhower and most essential to the operation of the Presidency are Sherman Adams, who as Assistant to the President is a full-fledged chief of staff; James C. Hagerty, who as Press Secretary stands guard over the channels of opinion to and from the President; Bernard M. Shanley, who has the uninviting task of handling the schedule of appointments; Major General Wilton B. Persons, who maintains liaison with Congress; Kevin McCann, who is in charge of preparing speeches and other public statements; and Gerald D. Morgan, Special Counsel to the President. Associated with these men are another half-dozen Assistants, some labeled "special," others "administrative," who cover a wide range of responsibility running from liaison with the states (Howard L. Pyle) through economic problems (Gabriel Hauge) to disarmament (Harold Stassen). In addition, the President has designated two officials with jobs of their own to serve him personally—Chairman Lewis L. Strauss of the Atomic Energy Commission and Chairman Philip Young of the Civil Service Commission. Finally, he has one aide for each of the armed services.

The National Security Council was established in 1947 "to advise the President with respect to the integration of domestic, foreign, and military policies relating to the national security." The current membership of the Council includes the President, the Vice-President, the Secretaries of State and Defense, and the Director of the Office of Defense Mobilization. The core of this interdepartmental committee is a permanent staff headed by an executive secretary, James S. Lay, Jr. Suspended from the National Security Council, although not an integral part of the Executive Office, is the Central Intelligence Agency. The Council, which usually invites other officials like the Joint Chiefs of Staff and Secretary of the Treasury to sit with it, is actually a specialized cabinet to advise the President in the whole field of foreign and military affairs. Its total personnel is about twenty-five.

The Council of Economic Advisers, a team of three economists aided by thirty staff and clerical aides, joined the presidential camp under the terms of the Employment Act of

1946, which directed it to assist and advise the President in the preparation of an annual economic report on the state of the Union; "gather timely and authoritative information concerning economic developments and economic trends" and submit studies based on this information to the President; "develop and recommend to the President national economic policies" designed to "promote maximum employment, production, and purchasing power"; and "make and furnish such studies, reports thereon, and recommendations with respect to matters of federal economic policy and legislation as the President may request." The breadth of this mandate affords Chairman Arthur F. Burns and his colleagues full opportunity to serve the President as a formalized "brain trust" in all matters that touch upon the economic state of the Union. Without it he could hardly be expected to be our Manager of Prosperity.

The Office of Defense Mobilization, established by Mr. Eisenhower himself in 1953, acts on behalf of the President "to direct, control, and coordinate all mobilization activities of the executive branch of the Government including but not limited to production, procurement, stabilization, and transport activities," and, of course, it advises the President on all these matters. Its director, Arthur S. Flemming, is aided in his protean task, which is now largely a question of planning, by a staff numbering about 300.

Last in line but far from least in importance, the Bureau of the Budget under its director, Percival F. Brundage, serves the President as an "administrative general staff." The Bureau is one of the two original components of the Executive Office, having been transferred in 1939 from the Treasury Department, and is sure to be functioning in much the same way when most other components have passed into history. Without it the President could not begin to do his job as Chief Executive. In addition to taking the burden of the budget almost completely off his back, it engages in a broad range of activities designed to achieve "more efficient and economical conduct of the Government service," assists in preparing the President's executive orders and proclamations, and acts as his clearinghouse for proposed legislation and enrolled bills. The Bureau counts 420 employees, and no one in his right mind has ever suggested that it could get along with any fewer.

In and around these five key agencies, especially the White House Office, swirls a whole galaxy of persons—Secretaries, Under Secretaries, committees of Secretaries, advisory boards of Under Secretaries, study groups, presidential commissions—who give some, most, or all of their time and best thoughts directly to the President. One of the features of the Executive Office is its plasticity, at least at the edges. The President is, as he should be, entirely free to divide his immediate burden among his assistants in his own way, to establish or disestablish interdepartmental committees or secretariats, to call on persons anywhere in the executive branch to perform special tasks, and, like all who preceded him, to take counsel with private citizens. If Mr. Eisenhower wants to use Sherman Adams as a chief of staff or put special trust in his Vice-President or revive the Cabinet as a coordinating agency, if he wants to take his television cues from Robert Montgomery or ask Willie Mays about juvenile delinquency or hold a White House Conference on Education, that is entirely his business. He runs his team in one way, each of the men he succeeded ran his in another, the men who succeed him will run theirs in ways yet unimagined.

At the same time, we must understand that the hard core of this machinery, especially the Bureau of the Budget, is now a permanent fixture in the national government. Many persons in it can look forward confidently to a long life of service for a long line of Presidents. Although those immediately around him are his personal choices, most of the men and women who serve them have tenure in their jobs. Although his personal touch is necessary to give the whole Executive Office its sense of direction, it could run for some time entirely on its own. The fact is that the Presidency has become "institutionalized." The President is still one man, but he is also, like any man with a thousand helpers, an institution. Most of the wheels go around steadily whether he watches them or not, as we learned so well during Mr. Eisenhower's illness. Many orders and suggestions and leaks emerge from "the White House" about which "the President" knows nothing. One must be especially careful today in reading newspapers to distinguish among what he says for himself, what his aides say for him, and what his aides say for themselves. If the distinction is not easy to make—and Washington is full of people who wish they could make it unerringly—that should remind us of the unity into which President, White House, and Executive Office finally merge.

I have already pointed out, with the help of Professor White, the momentous administrative significance of this development in the modern Presidency. Its constitutional significance, it seems to me, is even more momentous. It converts the Presidency into an instrument of twentieth-century government; it gives the incumbent a sporting chance to stand the strain and fulfill his constitutional mandate as a one-man branch of our three-part government; it deflates even the most forceful arguments, which are still raised occasionally, for a plural executive; it assures us that the Presidency will survive the advent of the positive state. Executive Order 8248 may yet be judged to have saved the Presidency from paralysis and the Constitution from radical amendment.

I trust it will be thought proper in a book of 175 pages on the Presidency to devote four or five to the Vice-Presidency, although even this ratio is no measure of the gap between them in power and prestige. The Presidency is the greatest constitutional office the world has known, a splendid chieftainship sought eagerly by just about every first-rate political figure in the nation, not to mention a horde of second-raters. The Vice-Presidency is a hollow shell of an office, an uncomfortable heir-apparency sought by practically no one we should like to see as President. It has perked up noticeably in the past eight years, but fundamentally it remains a disappointment in the American constitutional system.

The Vice-Presidency is one of our oldest problems. Some of the more astute members of the Convention of 1787 doubted that there was any need for a Vice-President, and Hamilton was forced to refute numerous criticisms of the office in *The Federalist*. There were apparently three reasons for creating the Vice-Presidency: to establish a constitutional heir for the President, to facilitate the selection of "continental characters" under the original electoral system, and to provide a presiding officer for the Senate not immediately devoted to the interests of any particular state. The framers also recognized the advantage of a moderator for this body with a deciding vote in the event of a tie. In general, they expected the office to be filled by the nation's number-two political figure, the man who had polled the second highest number of votes in the presidential election.

However cogent the reasons of the framers, and however high their expectations, the Vice-Presidency was a failure, and was recognized as such, almost from the outset. John Adams, the first to hold it, lamented that "my country has in its wisdom contrived for me the most insignificant office that ever the invention of man contrived or his imagination conceived." Thomas Jefferson, his successor, said something more meaningful than he realized when he described the "second office of government" as "honorable and easy," "the first" as "but a splendid misery." And several early statesmen referred to the Vice-President as "His Superfluous Excellency." The rise of the Federalist and Republican parties, the near disaster of the Jefferson-Burr election of 1800-1801, the consequent adoption of the Twelfth Amendment, and the establishment of the "Virginia Succession" all contributed to the decline of the office. The first two Vice-Presidents may have been John Adams and Thomas Jefferson, but the fifth and sixth were Elbridge Gerry and Daniel D. Tompkins; the seventh, John C. Calhoun, resigned to enter the Senate. And somewhere along the line there was a Vice-President named Throttlebottom—and a good one, too. Public men then, like public men today, apparently preferred misery with power to ease without it.

For the record, let me set down the powers of the Vice-President as they exist today. He draws two clear duties from the Constitution, to preside over the Senate and exercise a tie-breaking vote, and, as I count them, six from the laws: to appoint five midshipmen to the Naval Academy; to appoint four Senators to its Board of Visitors; to recommend two candidates to the President for appointment to the Military Academy; to sign enrolled bills and joint resolutions before they are sent to the President; to be a member of the Smithsonian Institution and its Board of Regents; and—the one grant of any consequence—to sit as a statutory member of the National Security Council. Occasionally he is designated to appoint several members to a special commission. He also draws his pay: $30,000 a year plus $10,000 for expenses.

These are dimensions of impotence, and impotence is the mark of a second-class office. Suspended in a constitutional limbo between executive and legislature, and in a political limbo between obscurity and glory, the Vice-Presidency has lost most of its significance as an instrument of government. Woodrow Wilson summed up the problem of the Vice-Presidency neatly when, in obvious exasperation, he wrote: "The chief embarrassment in discussing his office is, that in explaining how little there is to be said about it one has evidently said all there is to say."

The fact that the Vice-President has little to do is not in itself a danger spot in our constitutional system. In considering what he is, however, we must remember what he may be: President of the United States. John Adams, discerning as ever, remarked in the very first days: "I am possessed of two separate powers, the one *in esse* and the other *in posse*. I am Vice President. In this I am nothing, but I may be everything." The reality of vice-presidential impotence has generally loomed far more prominently in the nation's political consciousness than the possibility of a succession to the Presidency; the *esse* of the office has too often blotted out the *posse*. The real danger of the powerless Vice-Presidency is therefore this: that it is rarely occupied by a man for whom a majority of the people would have voted as a candidate for the Presidency. The potential importance of the Vice-President as heir apparent to the President, pointed up by seven successions in 167 years, has not been sufficient to attract leading political figures to seek it as a matter of course. Most men of ability and ambition would still rather be a leading Senator or Secretary of State than Vice-President, even after all the good and exciting times that Richard Nixon has had. While the office is not quite the political county farm that some of its critics have portrayed, few men of presidential stature have occupied it since Adams and Jefferson, and they usually had to be dragooned into accepting their party's nomination. We have had distinguished Vice-Presidents, but who since Van Buren has been second only to the President as a political figure, even of his own party? Mr. Dooley's creator echoed our opinion of most Vice-Presidents when he pleaded with Theodore Roosevelt not to go down in a submarine, and ended on the note, "Well, you really shouldn't do it—unless you take Fairbanks with you." Roosevelt had already added his bit to the lore of the Vice-Presidency by stating, "I would a great deal rather be anybody, say a professor of history, than Vice-President." The man who served under Wilson and longed for a good five-cent cigar, Thomas R. Marshall, went Roosevelt one better by describing himself as "a man in a cataleptic fit," who "is conscious of all that goes on but has no part in it," and then topped that by noting the propriety of his membership in the Smithsonian Institution, where he had "opportunity to compare his fossilized life with the fossils of all ages."

Like the Vice-Presidency itself, the danger of a third-rater as Vice-President is everything *in posse* and little *in esse*. Many a party hack has served his four years presiding over the Senate and passed into oblivion. On the other hand, several party hacks have succeeded to the Presidency with harmful results. Only one of the original reasons for this office is valid today—the necessity of a constitutional heir for the President, and it is exactly here that the Vice-Presidency has failed most conspicuously. The only ways to erase the danger spot are to eliminate the office or to make it a highly attractive place of honor and power. If the history of the Vice-Presidency means anything, the former course is inconceivable and the latter unlikely.

To the credit of both Presidents Truman and Eisenhower, the Vice-Presidency has experienced something of a renaissance in recent years. Alben Barkley was probably the most distinguished man nominated for the office since John C. Calhoun, and he proved extremely useful to Mr. Truman as a link to Congress. Richard Nixon, however—and I do not mean this disrespectfully—was hauled up to the second rung from far down the ladder for reasons that had nothing to do with his qualifications for the Presidency. Mr. Nixon, thanks to the President's mind and the President's heart, has been easily the busiest and most useful Vice-President within memory. Yet he is still inferior to Secretary of State Dulles or Speaker Rayburn or a dozen Senators in influence and prestige, and the Vice-Presidency is still very far from being in fact the "second office of the land." One of the few lessons we should have learned clearly from the anxious weeks following Mr. Eisenhower's heart attack was that the Vice-President, even when favored openly by the President, is unsuited to serve in emergencies as an "acting President"—unless, of course, the President's disability is clearly established. Sherman Adams, George Humphrey, John Foster Dulles, James Hagerty—all these men were more important and influential than Mr. Nixon in the conduct of the Presidency in those weeks. The weaknesses of the Vice-Presidency were never more dramatically exposed than at the moment when a bewildered nation turned to it for strength and guidance. Neither in law, custom, nor political circumstance was it prepared to assume the burden that many well-meaning citizens were trying to thrust upon it.

Mr. Nixon, to be sure, has made as much of a success of this frustrating office as any man could be expected to make. He has sat by invitation in the Cabinet and presided over it in the President's absence, sat by right in the National Security Council and taken part in decisions of great moment, relieved the President of any number of trips to the airport to greet distinguished visitors, served as chairman of the Committee on Government Contracts, visited several dozen countries as special envoy of the President, and acted as both trouble shooter and pacifier in executive-legislative relations. Most important of all, he stood for a few days—and stood with reserve and dignity—on the brink of the Presidency. Yet even then he was a thousand times bigger *in posse* than he was *in esse*.

Within the inherent limitations of the office, which have never been more apparent, the Vice-Presidency is generally what the President chooses to make it. President Eisenhower has chosen to make it something much more than it usually is, and Vice-President Nixon, unlike many of his predecessors, has been delighted to go along. It must be recognized, however, that no permanent solution to the problem has been worked, and I doubt very much that it can be. From time to time it is suggested that the Vice-President be converted into the President's top executive assistant—I once made such a proposal myself, which I hereby recant—but the road to this revolution would, I feel sure, prove rocky, dangerous, and finally impassable. The most we can hope for is that Congress will increase the Vice-President's emoluments, establish an official residency, and give him a staff of his own; that a series of Presidents will follow Mr. Eisenhower's lead and thus fix some of these recent departures in constitutional custom; and that the parties will seek consciously to nominate men who are qualified by experience, character, and prestige to succeed to the Presidency. It would be reassuring to know that from this time forward neither party would nominate a man to the second office who had not been considered seriously for the first. There is evidence that the people think a great deal more of it than do the politicians, and the latter should face up to the blunt fact that every time they select a candidate for the Vice-Presidency they are selecting one for the Presidency. It might be of interest to hear Mr. Eisenhower's testimony on this subject, delivered at a press conference in 1955:

Q. (by Mr. Reston of the New York *Times*) Mr. President . . . what I was trying to get at was what is your philosophy about the role of the nominee in the selection of the Vice-President? Is it your view that the convention is sovereign, it can pick anybody it likes, or should it, in your judgment, follow the recommendation of the Presidential nominee?

A. Well, I would say this, Mr. Reston: It seems obvious to me that unless the man were acceptable to the Presidential nominee, the Presidential nominee should immediately step aside. . . . If there isn't some kind of general closeness of feeling between these two, it is an impossible situation, at least the way I believe it should be run.

I personally believe the Vice-President of the United States should never be a nonentity. I believe he should be used. I believe he should have a very useful job.

Plainly, then, it is up to each future President—first as nominee, then as incumbent—to make whatever can be made of this disappointing office.

To return in conclusion to the Presidency, I have tried to indicate some of the major developments that lead many observers to believe that the office is in a period of pronounced transition. There were other developments to which I might have called attention—the blending of the President's roles as Chief Diplomat and Commander in Chief (to the advantage of each), the addition of new statutory emergency powers to his already large stock, the recasting of the presidential succession—but the five discussed in detail are evidence enough of this transition. His strong posture of legislative leadership, his new channels of opinion, his increased concern for peace and prosperity, his emergence as a leader in the struggle for personal liberty and racial equality, and above all his conversion into an institution—these are the fresh ingredients of the Presidency. If I may mix the metaphor, the foundations of the office remain as firm as ever, but there are some interesting changes going on in the superstructure.

CHAPTER 5

THE MODERN PRESIDENTS

☆

It has not been easy to suppress the giddy urge to spice this "cool examination" with comments about the men who have been in and around the Presidency during the past quarter-century, and now I am about to give way all at once. I do not give way merely to gratify a weakness for gossip about "the man in the White House." We cannot come to close grips with the modern Presidency as institution or as force in history unless we talk in highly personal terms about the men who have held it. Woodrow Wilson once remarked that "governments are what politicians make them, and it is easier to write of the President than of the Presidency." With his blessing I turn to the delicate but delightful task of judging the performances of Franklin D. Roosevelt, who created the modern Presidency, of Harry S. Truman, who defended it, and of Dwight D. Eisenhower, who inherited it and made it acceptable to the American people.

Let us place ourselves, if we can, on the throne of posterity, and from that serene point of vantage let us look back objectively—as we expect our great-grandchildren to look back —at the policies and achievements of each of these men. "Ranking the Presidents" has always been what A. A. Milne would have called a Favorite Indoor Sport of history-minded Americans, and I see no reason why we should not play it with Roosevelt, Truman, and Eisenhower as happily as we play it with Jackson, Cleveland, and Harding. I am especially concerned to anticipate the opinions of our descendants about the "greatness" of our last three Presidents. Will Roose-

velt be ranked with Lincoln or Wilson? Will Truman be
compared with Johnson or Theodore Roosevelt? Will the
old soldier named Eisenhower be placed just below the old
soldier named Washington or just above the old soldier
named Grant? Our answers to the following questions, which
historians like to ask about the Presidents long dead, may
help us to predict the judgments of posterity on each of
the Presidents in our time:

In what sort of times did he live? A man cannot possibly
be judged a great President unless he holds office in great
times. Washington's eminence arose from the founding of
the Republic, Jackson's from the upsurge of democracy,
Lincoln's from the Civil War, and Wilson's from World
War I. We have no right even to consider a man for membership in this exclusive club unless he, too, presides over the
nation in challenging years.

If the times were great, how bravely and imaginatively
did he bear the burden of extraordinary responsibility? A
successful President must do a great deal more than stand
quiet watch over the lottery of history: he must lead people,
Congress, and administration; he must make the hard decisions that have to be made, and make most of them correctly; he must work hard at being President and see that
these decisions are carried out.

What was his philosophy of presidential power? To be a
great President a man must think like a great President.
If he is not widely and persistently accused in his own time
of "subverting the Constitution," he may as well forget about
being judged a truly eminent man by future generations.

What sort of technician was he? How efficiently did he
organize his energies, direct his lieutenants, and thus exercise his powers? Lincoln could be an indifferent administrator and yet a great President, but the rise of the modern
state has made it impossible for an inefficient President
to discharge even a fraction of his duties with much hope
of success.

What men did he call on for help? If the modern Presidency,
as I have insisted, is irrevocably institutionalized, the modern

President cannot expect to accomplish much unless he surrounds himself with wise statesmen, shrewd politicians, and able technicians.

What manner of man was he beneath the trappings of office? We remember a President as much for his quirks and quips as for his deeds and decisions. If he is not the sort of man around whose person legends will arise in profusion, he will surely not meet the final test of presidential greatness: to be enshrined as a folk hero in the American consciousness.

What was his influence on the Presidency? We are not likely to rate a President highly if he weakens the office through cowardice or neglect. A place at the top of the ladder is reserved only for those strong Presidents who have added to the office by setting precedents for other strong Presidents to follow. Up to now, at least, the American people have generally equated "greatness" with "strength."

Finally, what was his influence on history? In particular, did he inspire or represent—and find words to explain—some massive readjustment in the pattern of American society? More than one President has been granted a high place in history because he sensed the direction of American democracy in his times and bent or hastened its onward course.

Before I hazard this informed guess about the future status of Roosevelt, Truman, and Eisenhower, let me remind my readers of one cardinal fact: American history is written, if not always made, by men of moderate views, broad interests, and merciful judgments. Time works for rather than against most Presidents. The men who write texts for our great-grandchildren, like the men who wrote them for us, will be concerned with broad accomplishments and failures, not with petty tales of corruption, ill temper, and intrigue, and I would hope that some of their spirit would rub off on this effort to anticipate them.

Franklin D. Roosevelt's times may well be judged to have been the most exciting and demanding in the history of

the Republic, as uncertain as the first fluid years under Washington, as hazardous as the first dark years under Lincoln.
We bestow the accolade of greatness on a President like
Wilson for having led the nation safely through one major
crisis. Franklin Roosevelt, who led us through two, must
therefore enjoy a long head start toward the eminence he
surely wished for in his heart. It would have been sufficient
unto posterity for him to have weathered the Hundred Days
and launched the New Deal. What can posterity do but
think grandly of a President who also led us into, through,
and very nearly out of the greatest war in history, and in
the midst of travail launched the United Nations? The
willingness of the American people to give Roosevelt a
third term and then a fourth is the most eloquent of all
witnesses to the glory of his times.

The essence of Roosevelt's Presidency was his airy eagerness to meet the age head on. Thanks to his flair for drama,
he acted as if never in all history had there been times like
our own. Thanks to his sense of history, he exulted in the
vast responsibilities that were thrust upon him even as he
sought them. In the first Hundred Days he gave Congress
a kind of leadership it had not known before and still does
not care to have repeated. In the golden days of the New
Deal he initiated a dozen massive programs designed to save
a society from the defects of its virtues. In the hard days
before Pearl Harbor he led us step by step to a war we always
knew we would have to fight, and in the harder but somehow
happier days thereafter he was a Commander in Chief no
less awesome than Lincoln himself.

His blunders and trimmings are all on record: the casual
manipulation of the dollar in 1933, the ill-conceived assault
upon the Court in 1937, the ill-starred interference in the
primaries in 1938, the shabby hesitation in the Spanish Civil
War, the offhand acquiescence in the evacuation of the
Japanese-Americans from the Pacific coast in 1942, the mis-
placed confidence in his own ability to "handle Stalin," the
shocking unconcern over the education of his Vice-President

in 1945, and above all the failure of the New Deal to achieve genuine economic recovery. Yet I have an idea that most of these will be driven from the memories of our posterity by his undoubted successes in launching T.V.A. and social security, swinging the Lend-Lease Program and the "Destroyer Deal," setting the grand strategy of the war, initiating the atom bomb project, and converting America into a bountiful arsenal for fifty countries in addition to his own. Nor are these earth-shaking events the whole story of his capacity for decision and leadership. When many of his acts as Commander in Chief are long forgotten, grateful men will remember that he was as devoted a conservationist as Theodore Roosevelt, as warm a friend of culture as Jefferson, and as ardent a free trader as any President who ever lived. We may never hear the end of arguments over the direction in which he led us, but few are left to argue that he preferred drifting to leading, at least in time of crisis. "He demonstrated the ultimate capacity to dominate and control a supreme emergency," Sumner Welles has written, "which is the rarest and most valuable characteristic of any statesman."

No sane observer has ever placed Franklin Roosevelt in the Buchanan line of Presidents. He was, to be sure, a constitutionalist, but his Constitution was that of Jackson, Theodore Roosevelt, Lincoln, and Wilson. Like the first of these he considered the independence of the office to be its most precious asset, like the second he thought of himself as a steward of the people, like the third he made himself a "constitutional dictator" in time of severe national emergency. The gamy flavor of his theory of presidential power may be tasted in some remarkable words delivered to Congress on September 7, 1942. In demanding the repeal of an inflationary provision in the Price Control Act of 1942 he stated flatly:

I ask the Congress to take this action by the first of October. Inaction on your part by that date will leave me with an inescapable responsibility to the people of this country to see to it that the war effort is no longer imperiled by threat of economic chaos.

In the event that the Congress should fail to act, and act adequately, I shall assume the responsibility and I will act. . . .

The President has the power, under the Constitution and Congressional acts, to take measures necessary to avert a disaster which would interfere with the winning of the war. . . .

The American people can be sure that I will use my powers with a full sense of my responsibility to the Constitution and to my country. The American people can also be sure that I shall not hesitate to use every power vested in me to accomplish the defeat of our enemies in any part of the world where our own safety demands such defeat.

When the war is won, the powers under which I act automatically revert to the people—to whom they belong.

Finally, like Wilson he considered himself a lay preacher to the American people. Just a few days after his first election he remarked:

The Presidency is not merely an administrative office. That is the least of it. It is pre-eminently a place of moral leadership.

All of our great Presidents were leaders of thought at times when certain historic ideas in the life of the nation had to be clarified. Washington personified the idea of Federal Union. Jefferson practically originated the party system as we know it by opposing the democratic theory to the republicanism of Hamilton. This theory was reaffirmed by Jackson.

Two great principles of our government were forever put beyond question by Lincoln. Cleveland, coming into office following an era of great political corruption, typified rugged honesty. Theodore Roosevelt and Wilson were both moral leaders, each in his own way and for his own time, who used the Presidency as a pulpit.

That is what the office is—a superb opportunity for reapplying, applying to new conditions, the simple rules of human conduct to which we always go back. Without leadership alert and sensitive to change, we are bogged up or lose our way.

Not more than two or three Presidents, it seems safe to say, ever took so broad a view of their powers as did Franklin D. Roosevelt.

Even his stoutest friends admit that Roosevelt was not much of an administrator. His working habits were casual, personal, and opportunistic; he permitted the inevitable feuds of an active administration to flare too hotly and run too long; he was unbelievably reluctant to discipline the feckless and fire the useless; he was an improviser who lacked the improviser's most essential quality—the candid courage to admit a failure and begin all over again. Yet it is possible that his friends give away too much to his enemies on this particular count. Governments bent on social reform are bound to be wasteful of time and money; Presidents who lead such governments have bigger things to think about than petty details of administration. Roosevelt was aware of his own shortcomings and took a bold step to correct the most glaring of them in Executive Order 8248, which I described in Chapter 4. Beyond that he did not care to go, for he chose to save his energies for his larger responsibilities as leader of the American people. A successful President is something more than a skilled administrator; it almost seems as if Roosevelt set out consciously to reverse the record of Hoover by being a second-rate administrator and a first-rate President. In the end, his deficiencies as an administrator were nearly swallowed up in his genius for bringing politics to the support of policy. A master politician, he never lost sight of a truth that James A. Farley has yet to perceive: that politics is only a game, and a shabby game at that, if it is not directed to larger and nobler ends. His generally masterful leadership of Congress was the most significant application of this truth.

In the course of two major crises and twelve strenuous years Roosevelt called on hundreds of able men to help him in his tasks. He called on some odd and disreputable characters, too, four or five of whom had no business being within fifty miles of the White House, but for the most part he displayed a remarkable talent for putting the right man in the right job. Harold Ickes as Secretary of the Interior, Jim Farley as chairman of the Democratic National Committee, David Lilienthal as head of T.V.A., Robert H. Jackson as Attorney General, Harold D. Smith as Director of the Budget, Sumner Welles as Under Secretary of State, Robert E. Sherwood and Samuel Rosenman as speech writers, and Stephen Early as Press Secretary are examples of what I mean by "the right man in the right job."

In time of war, when it was no longer necessary for the

President to confine his search for help to men of his own political stripe, this talent broadened into genius. It is easy to forget that Leahy, Marshall, King, Arnold, Eisenhower, Stimson, Vinson, Patterson, Land, McCloy, Knudsen, Forrestal, Winant, Nelson, Byrnes, Harriman, Donovan, and all the others were, in almost every instance, his personal choices to fill their critical positions. It is just as easy to forget that several of his appointments to the Supreme Court were extremely distinguished or that his elevation of Harlan Fiske Stone to the chief justiceship was an act of pure statesmanship. In the end, what impresses me most vividly about the men around Roosevelt is the number of flinty no-sayers who served him, loyally but not obsequiously, and the way in which he always remained "the boss." I think, in this regard, of Nathaniel Hawthorne's musing on Andrew Jackson, a President who was also thought to be inferior in intellect to the clever men surrounding him:

> Surely he was a great man, and his native strength, as well of intellect as of character, compelled every man to be his tool that came within his reach; and the more cunning the individual might be, it served only to make him the sharper tool.

Roosevelt is already well on his way to enshrinement as folk hero—although to be sure, he will have to double as folk devil for at least another fifty years. Those millions who still hate him lavishly may as well face the hard fact bravely that their great-grandchildren's children will read with affectionate interest of the bird walks on the Hudson, the manly training under Dr. Peabody, and the dogged triumph over crippling pain. His virtues and faults are either too well known or too bitterly contested for me to review in this short space, but I would like to point to several qualities that made him a man for posterity to remember: his buoyancy, which made it possible for him to love the job as no other President except the first Roosevelt had loved it; his breadth of vision, which, in time of war, gave him a clearer grasp of America's productive potential than the leaders of industry seemed to have themselves; his delight in danger, which made him a natural leader for a generation whose lot was, as a critic remarked, "one damned crisis after another"; his sense of history, which invited him even before his inauguration to join the company of Presidents to whom monuments are raised long after their death; and his personal conservatism, which provided a solid base for his political liberalism and kept it from running beyond the aspirations of the American people. (To those who doubt the existence or influence of this last quality, I recommend a trip through the old house at Hyde Park.) Roosevelt will never, I am sure, be ranked with Washington and Lincoln, for there were touches of softness and mummery about him that will keep him from sainthood. If he was as busy as Rabbit and as bouncy as Tigger, he was too often, I fear, as big a bluffer as Owl.

Roosevelt's influence on the Presidency was tremendous. Only Washington, who made the office, and Jackson, who remade it, did more than he to raise it to its present condition of strength, dignity, and independence. I often wonder if Mr. Eisenhower realizes how many of the powers and privileges he commands, and how much of the respect and assistance he enjoys, are a direct legacy from Franklin Roosevelt. The press conference, the Executive Office, the right to reorganize his administration, and the powers to protect industrial and financial peace are all parts of this legacy. Generals obey him, Congress defers to him, and leaders of other nations honor him far more readily than they would had Roosevelt not been so forceful a President. Like every such President he left his successor to reap the wild wind, and in at least one instance, the passage of the Twenty-second Amendment, the reaction to his high-riding incumbency was sufficiently angry to weaken the office permanently. Yet the verdict of history will surely be that he left the Presidency a more splendid instrument of democracy than he found it.

His influence on history is something for our descendants to assess. They will know firsthand, as we can only guess from afar, whether the two great "revolutions" he set in motion turned out to be blessings or curses for the American people. The first of these was the New Deal, which was essentially a decision to preserve American capitalism by invoking the positive power of the national government to support and stabilize the economy. Roosevelt, the master of public opinion, found the words to rationalize this vast readjustment in our ways of thinking and doing. He will long be remembered, fondly by some, contemptuously by others, for having read the word "security" into the American definition of "liberty."

The second great change took form in the coalition of warring powers and the plans for the United Nations, both of which involved a series of decisions aimed at plunging America permanently, for America's own sake, into world affairs. Roosevelt's skill with words was again equal to the high occasion, and men in every land will quote them for centuries to come. We must not forget that his record in war and diplomacy made him a giant figure in world as well as in American history. If we fail to honor him, other men will do it for us—as Winston Churchill honored him in the House of Commons:

> Of Roosevelt, however, it must be said that had he not acted when he did, in the way he did, had he not felt the generous surge of freedom in his heart, had he not resolved to give aid to Britain, and to Europe in the supreme crisis through which we have passed, a hideous fate might well have overwhelmed mankind and made its whole future for centuries sink into shame and ruin. It may well be that the man whom we honor today not only anticipated history, but altered its course, and altered it in a manner which has saved the freedom and earned the gratitude of the human race.

This has been much too simple a review of a complicated man and his turbulent times, but it would be capricious of me not to end by registering my opinion, to which I did not come easily, that Franklin Roosevelt is fixed firmly in the hierarchy of great Presidents alongside Jackson and Wilson, a small step above Theodore Roosevelt and Jefferson, a sizable step, which may grow smaller over the years, below Washington and Lincoln. He had his own rendezvous with history, and history will be kind to him.

Harry S. Truman presents a much tougher case for objective evaluation than does Franklin D. Roosevelt. At times he had the look of greatness, at times he gave off—and still gives off, to the delight of the working press—the sound of meanness. But lest we prejudge him too easily and emotionally, let us subject him to our eight tests of presidential greatness. In so doing, I would recall my warning—which is especially pertinent to his amazing Presidency—that history is written, if not always made, by men of moderate views.

His times were not so laden with drama and hazard as those of Franklin Roosevelt, but they were at least as decisive for the American future as those of Jefferson and Wilson. He, too, has a head start for glory, a point that his most savage detractors must concede in his favor. In his two terms we passed through a whole series of nagging crises. We had decadence and destruction prophesied for us again and again. Yet on January 20, 1953 we still stood before the world a free, prosperous, liberty-loving people with no more wounds and neuroses than we probably deserved. History may record that it was no mean achievement simply to have gone through the motions of being President in these eight years. This fact alone will surely elevate Mr. Truman above Pierce and Coolidge and quite probably above Polk and Cleveland.

The larger fact is that Harry Truman, once he had got the bearings that Roosevelt neglected to give him, did a great deal more than go through the motions of forwarding messages to Congress, greeting kings and Eagle Scouts, paying political debts, and saying "no comment" to the press. He studied, read, conferred, and dictated as long and hard as any President who ever lived, and he faced up to at least a dozen decisions that gave the world a hard shake. He, too, has a record of sins of commission and omission, especially in domestic affairs. In the former category, I would list his proposal to draft the railroad strikers in 1946 and his seizure of the steel industry in 1952, in the latter his offhand manner toward painful evidence of subversion, corruption, and shoddiness in high places. Yet these must certainly fade into obscurity before the dropping of the first atom bomb, the pursuit of nuclear research and production on a massive scale, the Truman Doctrine and the Berlin airlift, the Marshall Plan and NATO, and the decision to resist in Korea. Not one of his grave steps in foreign and military affairs, not even the questionable manner of dropping the bombs on Hiroshima and Nagasaki, has yet been proved wrong, stupid, or contrary to the best judgment and interests of the American people. He took all of them as the people expect their President to take such fateful steps: resolutely, solemnly, and hopefully. Truman rarely if ever had Roosevelt's sure touch of leadership, perhaps because he often appeared dizzy from the speed of his ride to the top, but there is small disposition among either his admirers or detractors to hold anyone but him responsible for his actions.

Truman came in time to an even more exalted view of the Presidency than did Roosevelt. His spacious understanding of its powers and obligations will surely impress posterity more than his disturbing lapses from decorum. Certainly no President ever spoke so grandly and yet humbly of his authority. Certainly no President ever gave a more imaginative and accurate description of his job:

> And people talk about the powers of a President, all the powers that a Chief Executive has, and what he can do. Let me tell you something—from experience!
>
> The President may have a great many powers given to him in the Constitution and may have certain powers under certain laws which are given to him by the Congress of the United States; but the principal power that the President has is to bring people in and try to persuade them to do what they ought to do without persuasion. That's what I spend most of my time doing. That's what the powers of the President amount to.

An entirely new theory of the Presidency can be spun out of that folksy statement, which Truman repeated with amusing variations on at least a dozen occasions.

If he did not always show himself sufficiently aware of

the limitations of his office, it must be remembered that less impetuous men than he—Lincoln, Wilson, and Franklin D. Roosevelt—might also have considered themselves empowered to seize the steel mills in 1952. In any case, for all his alleged lack of learning and of disposition for reflection, Mr. Truman demonstrated a more clear-cut philosophy of presidential power than any predecessor except Woodrow Wilson. The heaviest black mark against his reading of the Presidency, in my opinion, was his cavalier disregard of the sensibilities and prerogatives of Congress in the harsh debate of 1951 over the power to station troops in Europe. His failure to associate Congress more quickly and positively in the Korean War and his partisan seizure of the steel mills were hardly less censurable.

As a technician Truman had few equals in the long history of the Presidency. Most experienced students of public administration agree that he organized his time, which meant a seventy-hour week, and distributed his energies, which were legendary, with the sure touch of the professional. Yet he was not a professional at all, which is another way of saying that he learned his job on the job with astounding success. On several counts he is open to severe criticism: his methods of dealing with Congress were inexcusably irritating; he permitted raw politics to hold sway in areas to which it should have been rigidly denied entry; the moral tone of his administration unsettled even some of his most devoted admirers. Yet in the White House itself things were remarkably serene and efficient. The conjunction of cold war, which threw a hundred new burdens on an already overburdened office, and Mr. Truman, who learned to delegate his own authority as well as any President in this century, speeded and made secure the institutionalization of the American Presidency. To those around him he was the very model of a modern executive.

One final point might illustrate both his technical competence and his awareness of his responsibilities. At the very moment when his stature seemed at its lowest, when he seemed to many Americans to have surrendered all sense of dignity or authority, Mr. Truman did something that not a single President in history had cared to do: with efficient grace he transferred power and information to an incoming administration of the opposite political party. From this time forward outgoing Presidents will be expected to assist incoming Presidents in the image of his high-minded co-operation with Dwight D. Eisenhower.

The roll call of those whom Truman enlisted in his staff and ranks runs the whole scale of virtue and talent from selfless greatness to dishonest incompetence. It has been suggested by some observers, and I am inclined to agree, that he made a more or less conscious deal with himself to insist upon nonpartisan excellence in military and diplomatic affairs and to tolerate partisan mediocrity in domestic affairs. The names of Marshall, Lovett, Forrestal, Acheson, Bedell Smith, Hoffman, Bohlen, Symington, Foster, Bradley, Clay, Lewis Douglas, Kennan, Draper, Jessup, Harriman, Finletter, Patterson, McCloy—and of Eisenhower and Dulles—are proof enough that Truman mobilized even more talent than Roosevelt in the areas that touch upon survival. The names of McGrath, McGranery, Snyder, Caudle, and Sawyer should be enough to remind us that the rest of the nation's business was carried on with little distinction and much bumbling. To complete a group portrait that has General Marshall sitting on one side of the President and General Vaughan on the other, I think we may say with sorrowful conviction that Truman's appointments to the Supreme Court were about the least distinguished in history.

Harry S. Truman is a man whom history will delight to remember. Those very lapses from dignity that made him an object of scorn to millions of Republicans—the angry letters, testy press conferences, whistle stops, and impossible sport shirts—open his door to immortality. It is a rare American, even a rare Republican, who can be scornful about a man one hundred years dead, and our descendants will be chuckling over his Missouri wit and wisdom long after the "five-percenters" have been buried and forgotten. They will read with admiration of the upset he brought off in 1948,

with awe of the firing of General MacArthur, and with a
sense of kinship of the way he remained more genuinely
"plain folks" than any other President. They will be moved
by the simple dignity of his confession: "There are probably
a million people in this country who could do the presidential
job better than I, but I've got the job and I'm doing the
very best I can." He was fascinating to watch, even when
the sight hurt, and he will be fascinating to read about. The
historians can be expected to do their share to fix him securely
in history, for he provides a classic case study of one of
their favorite themes: the President who grows in office.

Truman's influence on the Presidency can be summed
up in the simple judgment that he was a highly successful
Andrew Johnson. The Presidency had grown enough in
Franklin Roosevelt's time to satisfy most Americans for
at least another generation; it was his successor's high duty
to see that the new tools of democratic leadership were not
blunted or stolen by the forces of reaction. This duty Mr.
Truman discharged with enthusiasm and success. He defended the integrity of the Presidency stoutly against the
grand challenge of MacArthur and the sabotage of McCarthy,
and even after his departure he defended it against the
vulgar showmanship of Representative Velde. Whatever
damage he did to the office by intruding too one-sidedly into
labor disputes or by insulting Congress gratuitously or by
losing control of some of his subordinates was altogether
temporary in effect. The office he handed over to Eisenhower
was no less magnificent than the office he inherited from
Roosevelt, and this may well be considered a remarkable
achievement.

There appear to have been two great events in Truman's
eight years for which he may be remembered as Madison
or Grant or Taft or Hoover will never be remembered. One
was domestic in character—the first real beginnings of a
many-sided program toward eliminating discrimination and
second-class citizenship in American life. The other was international—the irrevocable commitment of the American
people to active co-operation with other nations in search

of world peace and prosperity. Over neither of these vast beginnings did Mr. Truman exercise much control, yet to each he gave the full support of the Presidency. He will surely be remembered, and may yet be supremely honored, for the President's Committee on Civil Rights and the resulting message to Congress of February 2, 1948. He will as surely be remembered, and as possibly supremely honored, for his actions in support of collective security against Communist aggression. It was a grand accomplishment in the total sweep of American history to take this nation into its first peacetime military alliance (NATO), to commit us for the first time to defend an area in which we had no obvious national interest (the Greek-Turkish program), to meet Communist force with force of our own making (Korea, 1950), and to call for a long-range constructive program that could open the gate to world peace (Point Four). The Marshall Plan is also credited to his account.

Mr. Truman often remarked that equal opportunity for all Americans and lasting peace for all men were the two consuming goals of his administration. The achievement of these goals—if we are blessed enough to achieve them—must inevitably add luster to his name. His uncompromising opponents are certain that both courses—civil rights and internationalism—will lead us to disaster. As Truman himself often reminded us, we must all wait for history to judge between him and Governor Byrnes in the struggle for equal opportunity, and between him and Senator McCarthy in the search for peace with freedom. My feeling is that he may wait with confidence.

On the basis of this evidence I am ready to hazard an opinion, to which I also did not come easily or lightly, that Harry S. Truman will eventually win a place as President, if not as hero, alongside Jefferson and Theodore Roosevelt. There will be at least a half-dozen Presidents strung out below him who were more able and large-minded, but he had the good fortune to preside in stirring times and will reap large credit for having survived them. I cannot, in good conscience, predict greatness for his name. Certain deficiencies of intellect and perception must bar him from the seats of the mighty. We must remember that his consuming hobby has always been political and military history. He knew that there was a game called "Ranking the Presidents"; he confessed repeatedly and with a candor that embarrassed his listeners that he was an accident of history who did not belong on the ladder at all. Despite or because of this harsh self-appraisal, he made a determined effort to climb the ladder by imitating the well-remembered Presidents of the past and by acting beyond his gifts. Now that his climbing days are over and his reminiscing days have begun, he is a good deal less inclined to be harsh on himself.

He, too, will be a well-remembered President because he proved that an ordinary man could fill the world's most extraordinary office with devotion and high purpose. He may serve as a lasting symbol of the noble truth that gives strength and meaning to the American experiment: plain men *can* govern themselves; democracy *does* work. And his epitaph will read: he was distressingly petty in petty things; he was gallantly big in big things.

It may well seem the height of folly to attempt the long view of Dwight D. Eisenhower. He is still President, and we have practically no perspective on him. He is willing to be President again—or at least three-fourths a President—and the fact that he is running for office means that neither he nor we will be at our best until the day after the election. It is possible that he is not yet past the half-way mark of his presidential course, and for the reputation of most notable Presidents the second term has been more decisive than the first. No one-term President except the martyred Lincoln has been honored with the accolade of greatness. Still, this is one of those games that are fun to play even on a muddy field and a murky day, and so let us ask our eight questions about President Eisenhower.

His times are less exacting than Roosevelt's or Truman's—and for this state of affairs we may well give thanks. While the threats of Communist marauding and domestic dislocation are always there beneath the surface, we have moved a long way out of the valley of tension since 1947 or 1950. If the President has his way during the rest of his time, we will move even farther out of the valley and deeper into the pleasant fields where men dream of perpetual peace and live beyond their record incomes. For all his bold talk in 1952 about a crusade, we knew—and if we did not know it then, we know it now—that his mission was to bring us peace at home and abroad. We were weary of reform in the one area and of adventure in the other, and we elected a President who would give us a breathing spell from both without taking us back over the ground we had already covered. Almost by definition, then, the times are the kind in which a President may win fame and gratitude but not immortality. Eisenhower has not been cut off completely from greatness by the nature of his times and mission, but he, like Theodore Roosevelt, must travel farther and faster in search of it. And as a gradualist in a time of gradualism, he has never really put his heart in the attempt. He has very little sense of history to begin with; and even if he had it to the full measure of Harry S. Truman, he is too modest to do an imitation of one of the earthshakers.

His manner of meeting his responsibilities, which are still huge by the old standards, is that of the moderate conservative he professes to be. In some domestic areas—for example, that of labor-management relations—he has been spared the nasty necessity of acting at all. In others—for example, the elimination of corruption in high places—he has been largely content to govern by setting a tone for others to match as best they can, and by cutting a man loose when he has made too unpleasant a mess. To his credit are the measures against recession in 1954 and his continued alertness in this field, the steady pressure in word and deed against racial discrimination, and the vastly improved administration of the defense budget. To his debit are the blunder of Dixon-Yates, the continued injustices and inanities of the loyalty-security program, the miscalculation of the public interest in the broad fields of conservation and regulation, and the untidy handling of the government's obligations in the polio vaccine fiasco. More serious than this, his total performance during the first year in office was that of a man who had apparently never heard of Sancho Panza's wise counsel that the essence of good government is "to make a good beginning."

In foreign affairs he has been, on his own terms, something of a master. His leadership has been conservative, and therefore more negative than what we were accustomed to receive from his predecessors, but he leaves no doubt in our minds that he is in command—except perhaps when Mr. Dulles speaks as sounding brass. Certainly he has come a long way back from the degrading days of Cohn and Schine and a long way up from the self-dug pit of Quemoy and Matsu. We have as satisfactory a peace as we could possibly expect in Korea; we are not bogged down in the morass of French colonialism; we have been to the Summit and heard our President speak out for peace as only he can do; we have taken the lead, thanks to his simple faith, in bringing the atom to the service of all mankind. We are still in a moral and economic position, if we will use it shrewdly, to beat the Soviet Union roundly in the new game of competitive coexistence. Men may well debate whether the leadership of this Republican President was given a check or a boost by the loss of his congressional majority in 1954, but no one can deny that he has taken steps toward peace in the last two years that no Democrat would have been permitted to take. No one can wave the bloody shirt of treason at Dwight D. Eisenhower, even when he exchanges notes with Marshal Zhukov and initiates negotiations with Red China. The thought has apparently occurred to many independent voters that the best formula yet devised for peace is a Republican President named Eisenhower and a Democratic Congress led by Johnson, George and Rayburn. Many of these voters, to be sure, are waiting to see if the formula need also include an heir apparent named Nixon and a Secretary of State named Dulles.

Eisenhower came to the Presidency with practically no

thoughts of his own about its powers and purposes. He came, moreover, as a Republican, and therefore committed, if that is the word, to the Whig theory of a partnership between President and Congress in which the latter sets the nation's goals without much help from the former. He had swallowed a good deal of the propaganda directed at Roosevelt and Truman, and the result was a first year in office during which his view of his powers was not much different from that announced long ago by William Howard Taft. Since the late fall of 1953 he has broadened this view considerably. He is still no Roosevelt or Truman, and he does not ever intend to be one. Nothing is more revealing of his philosophy of presidential power than his request early in 1955 for authority to defend Formosa and the Pescadores. It is obvious that Eisenhower, quite unlike Truman, considers the President to be under stern moral obligation to ask approval of Congress—certainly when there is time to ask it—for the use of powers in the twilight zone between them. Speaker Rayburn was among those who wondered aloud if this request would not cripple the striking power of the Presidency in a sudden crisis, but the point seemed to trouble Mr. Eisenhower not at all. In any case, he is much less impressed with his authority than was either of his Democratic predecessors, and if this, too, is a brake on his progress toward the stature of a great President, he does not appear to be overly worried. He may well think that posterity is for once ready to acclaim a President who saw no threat to his own position in being polite to Congress.

Eisenhower's competence as a technician is a subject of hot dispute. His supporters insist that he has moved beyond Roosevelt and Truman in distributing the routine burdens of the Presidency efficiently among an industrious and loyal team. His critics reply that he apparently learned the lesson of his army days much too thoroughly, for he has delegated not only the use but the control of some of his highest prerogatives and has lost his freedom of maneuver to an outsized, self-directing staff. From the very beginning, they say, he has reigned too much and ruled too little; indeed, the

"Eisenhower regency" began to function long before September 24, 1955.

The truth, I think, rests largely with his friends. The Presidency is at least as efficiently organized as it was in the best days of Harry Truman, and by delegating responsibility on a broad and imaginative scale the President himself has gained more hours for his own use than either of his predecessors enjoyed. Far more important in the light of history, his plans and methods—and a touch of Eisenhower luck—made it possible for the Presidency to run for weeks without a President and without a hitch. The main fire of his critics must be directed against the use he has made of his extra hours, although some might also be directed against his too-ready reliance on his own team for information and advice. He should keep the back door open to callers of his own choosing, and he really should devote one of those pleasant evening hours to reading the newspapers. Be all this as it may, he has done himself and the Presidency a great service by carrying the process of institutionalization at least a step and a half farther than Truman. If he has gone too far in surrendering control of some of his powers, the next President will have no trouble recovering it. As to his handling of Congress, few will argue that it has been anything but shrewd. The bipartisan support that he took to Geneva, which had even the most veteran reporters scratching their heads in wonder, was both a product of and a tribute to his unique brand of leadership.

The men around Eisenhower, like the men around Truman and Roosevelt, present a composite picture of all the virtues and most of the faults of public life. If there is less vision and daring and humor among those who now run the country, there is also more probity and frugality and attention to the business at hand. The President has not even come close to keeping his campaign promise to mobilize "the best brains in America," but how could he, a career soldier, have known that his freedom of choice would be narrowed so drastically by Republican politics and American folkways? Not only was he pledged in ways he could barely understand to concentrate on "jobs for the boys" rather than "boys for the jobs"; his, after all, was a business-man's government, and businessmen are understandably more reluctant than, let us say, professors to drop everything and rush to their President's call. It seems plain that Eisen-hower will not be especially remembered for the talents he assembled about him. He has been clearly more successful in finding the right men for his immediate staff than for the great offices of state. Adams, Hagerty, Burns, Hauge, Shanley, Dodge, Stassen, and Anderson are a far better team in their own league than the department heads are in theirs. Two final points can be made in the President's favor: his appointments to the Court have been vastly superior to Truman's; his Cabinet, which has undergone only two changes, is one of the most stable in American history. (Many observers feel that it has been much too stable.)

About the man himself there is nothing to say that has not been said a thousand times, except that despite his unique hold on the people of this country—or perhaps be-cause of it—he is less likely than Roosevelt to project his personality forcefully on the consciousness of history. A President who is adored by a little more than half the people and despised by the rest is a more probable candidate for immortality than a President who is liked by all of us in the center and disliked only by those on the fringes. Those very qualities of affability and decency that make him exactly the man the people want at this restful stage in their pilgrimage may be woven by time into a curtain of indiffer-ence that will hang darkly between our posterity and our most popular President. Eisenhower's character is not above criticism. Certainly no scholar can look with delight at the oc-casional surfacings of the current of anti-intellectualism that flows beneath the President's love of all mankind. Certainly no observer can fail to be troubled by the gap that often exists between what the President says and what he does about reducing tariffs or protecting our natural heritage or playing fair with those accused of disloyalty. Yet it cannot be doubted that his character, like his life, is an amazingly accurate projection of much of what is best in the American dream. He is charming, manly, brave, honest, capable, democratic, fair-minded, and incredibly lucky—and who, asks Leonard Hall complacently, who could ask for anything more?

During Eisenhower's first year it often seemed that his influence on the Presidency would be harmful, if not disastrous. It was not so much his unwillingness to exercise his legitimate prerogatives that troubled students of the Presidency, but rather his indifference to an unruly Congress celebrating the end of twenty years of "executive encroachment" with some encroachments of its own. Some time in 1953 Eisenhower came to an understanding of the modern Presidency, and since then he has been, if not a "strong" President, certainly a firm one. The manner of his tenure now appears to have been a blessing for the office, for in his own quiet way he has introduced many of the precedents of Roosevelt and Truman, about which the touch of crisis or partisanship still lingered, into the normal pattern of the Presidency. To put the matter another way, the Presidency called loudly for a Republican in 1952, for not until the Republicans had learned by experience that Whiggery was obsolete could the modernization of the Presidency be considered complete. Eisenhower has been a strong enough President to hold the line that his predecessors had staked out, but not too strong to lose touch with the Whigs in his party and thus miss this wonderful chance to educate them. We may go beyond this general observation to give him credit for these specific actions: his decisive opposition to the Bricker Amendment, his efforts to save the Cabinet from further decline, his reinvigoration of the National Security Council, his further refinement of the press conference, and his gallant attempt to do something with the Vice-President if not with the Vice-Presidency. All in all, it was a long journey uphill from 1953 and his needless surrenders to "the courtesy of the Senate" to 1955 and his bold announcement that he would ignore a provision of an act he had just signed—

because he, the President, thought the provision unconstitutional.

Since Mr. Eisenhower may be far from done with the Presidency, his influence on history is impossible to predict. The one question that history will insist that he answer successfully before admitting him to immortality is this: Can he go on in the next four years—assuming that he is asked to go on—to lay a solid foundation for several generations of peace? If peace does "break out" and stay with us for many years, surely he will be remembered fondly by a grateful world. We can now say no more than this: He has made a beginning, in deed as well as in word, and in making it he has done much to restore dignity and luster to the American image abroad. Some of the dignity and luster, one is bound to say, was lost during his first two years in office.

Yet even if he cannot do much more than he has done for peace, he may have already earned himself a special place in history for his leadership of that difficult but essential minority, the Republican party. He has not succeeded as much as he might have liked in remolding it in his own image of responsible conservatism, but he has persuaded most of its leaders to follow him into the twentieth century. By a route that often seemed much too circuitous but had a final logic of its own, he has brought the Republican party, and with it the business community, very near to accepting once and for all the ground rules of the New Economy and the burdens of the New Internationalism. And in doing this he has, as the columnists like to put it, "widened the center" so much that the country is basking in a climate of unity it has not enjoyed for thirty years or more.

Dissension and progressivism have their uses, too, just as surely as unity and conservatism, and men must now decide whether one term of a President like Eisenhower—a President who plainly prefers to let problems resolve themselves—is enough or too little. Win or lose, and the odds in the forthcoming election seem to be with him, this President has done a job that the American people wanted to have done, and history ought to make a special effort to remember him for it. I cannot emphasize too strongly that it usually prefers to ignore the President who promises peace rather than progress. Yet Eisenhower's conservatism has obviously been of a newer and higher order than that of McKinley or Taft or Coolidge, and it is possible that he may be richly honored for it, especially if he could quicken the pace of his administration sufficiently in a second term to soften the mounting tensions in education, race relations, and agriculture. It is possible, too, that the credentials of presidential greatness may be revised in the next generation to permit an occasional earth-smoother to sit in glory with the earth-shakers. Eisenhower already stands above Polk and Cleveland, and he has a reasonable chance to move up to Jefferson and Theodore Roosevelt. To label this President another Grant is merely absurd. We shall all say a lot of silly things for or against Eisenhower before this campaign is over, but we really should let General Grant rest in peace.

It would seem useful to conclude by drawing a few impersonal lessons from this exercise in personality. I propose, therefore, with only the barest comment, to list certain qualities that a man must have or cultivate if he is to be an effective modern President. In this instance I am more concerned with success than with greatness, with the needs of our contemporaries than with the judgments of our descendants. This is not a catalogue of every habit and talent we should hope for in our President. Like most Americans, I should be delighted if he would practice, faithfully but not self-righteously, all those virtues celebrated in the New Testament, *The Compleat Gentleman, The Way to Wealth,* and the handbook of the Boy Scouts of America. It can go without my saying that we like our President to be brave, clean, and honest. My list of stocks is short, but each item on it pays rich dividends:

Bounce: Not only must the President be healthy, in the sense of freedom from ailments; he must have that extra elasticity, given to few men, which makes it possible for him to thrive on the toughest diet of work and responsibility in the world. We may rightly expect to hear this point debated thoroughly in the campaign of 1956—now that Mr. Eisenhower himself, with characteristic candor, has laid the question before the American people.

Affability: The President's heart must be not only stout but warm. He must care deeply about people in the flesh, show an unfeigned interest in everything from dogs to the Dodgers, be willing to live his private life publicly, and have the sure instincts of the democrat. The Presidency is a people's office, and there is no room in it now for a man with ice in his veins.

Political skill: We used to hear a lot of wailing about men who were "too high-minded ever to be nominated and elected" but who none the less "would make excellent Presidents." If this was ever true, it is true no longer. The man who lacks the little arts to be elected President lacks the little arts to be President. How can he persuade people to do "what they ought to do without persuasion" if he cannot persuade them first of all to give him the job?

Cunning: We do not openly admire this quality, and too much of it can destroy the most dedicated man. Yet a President cannot get the best out of the dozens of able figures around him or keep them under his command unless he is a master in the delicate art of manipulating men.

A sense of history: This cast of mind raises him above all those around him, sobering yet exalting him with the thought that he sits in Lincoln's seat. No man or combination of men can match his power to influence history, and his grasp of this stark truth can save him from going astray into the fields of petty strife. It can save him, too, when he must act arbitrarily, from the backlash of opinion. There is practically nothing a President may decide to do in a moment of crisis that Washington or Jackson or Lincoln, or often Harding and Coolidge, did not already do in a similar spot.

The newspaper habit: The modern President must be on guard lest he be made a prisoner in his own house. He needs badly to know what people are thinking about events and about his handling of them. If he values his independence, he must have clear channels to the outside, and there is no substitute—certainly not a one-page digest of news and opinion prepared by his own secretaries—for a front page of the New York *Times* or the Chicago *Tribune,* an editorial in the St. Louis *Post-Dispatch* or the New York *Daily News,* a cartoon by Herblock or Fitzpatrick, a column by the Alsops or Pearson, or a magisterial lecture on the Constitution by Lippmann or Krock. An occasional half-hour in the appendix of the *Congressional Record* is an experience no President should miss.

A sense of humor: If he reads the *Record* and the *Tribune* at all faithfully, he will need a thick skin and a light heart. At least two recent Presidents have testified convincingly that they could not have survived in office if they had been unable to laugh at the world and themselves. It is remarkable how many of our admitted failures in the Presidency were men who could not chuckle at an unfriendly cartoon, much less frame the original for hanging in the President's study—a happy practice engaged in by several of our admitted successes.

Any one of these habits or talents can be a snare to a President who turns to it too often and confidently, but so, too, can almost every virtue in the American catalogue. The most we can hope for is a man who blends self-confidence and self-restraint in the balanced attitude that all our successful Presidents have struck. In the end, perhaps, it is essential (if far from enough) for him simply to look the part. Woodrow Wilson took hold of a momentous truth when he remarked in awe: "The office is so much greater than any man could honestly imagine himself to be that the most he can do is look grave enough and self-possessed enough to seem to fill it."

CHAPTER 6

THE PRESIDENCY RECONSIDERED

☆

We need no gift of prophecy to predict a long and exciting future for the American Presidency. There are those who dream of a President in the image of Calvin Coolidge; there are those who fear that the Presidency will be sapped by "the assaults of ignorance and envy." Neither the dream nor the fear is likely to find much substance in coming events. All the massive political and social forces that brought the Presidency to its present state of power and glory will continue to work in the future. Our economy and society will grow more rather than less interdependent, and we will turn to the President, anxiously if not always confidently, for help in solving the problems that fall thickly upon us. Our government will become more rather than less involved in the affairs of "mankind, from China to Peru," and the peoples of the world will look to its executive head for bold and imaginative leadership. Emergencies will grow nastier, Congress will become more unwieldy, and politics will take on more and more the spirit of a vast town meeting. And surely we have not seen our last great man in the White House. The people of the United States are no longer interested in presidential aspirants who promise only to be meek and mild. In the foreseeable future, as in the recent past, they will expect and get a full measure of presidential leadership. There is a Presidency in our future, and it is the Presidency of Jackson and Lincoln rather than of Monroe and Buchanan, of Roosevelt and Eisenhower rather than of Harding and Coolidge.

Since the Presidency of the future will grow out of the Presidency of the present, it is imperative to go one step farther with this appraisal. The total picture of the office drawn in this book has been perhaps more cheerful than it should be. In attempting to point up sharply the elements of strength and reliability in the Presidency, I have passed too lightly over problems and weaknesses to which some of our most useful public servants and astute political scientists have addressed themselves with fervor and ingenuity. Let me now turn to examine the most pressing of these. This is not, be it noted, an appraisal of the American system of government, even less of American society. I must assume that we have the society we deserve; I do assume that it would be neither possible nor sensible to alter the main outlines of our government. I propose to concentrate on the Presidency as it is and might be constituted, and to call attention to those defects, real or alleged, about which men of good will and good sense are most earnestly agitated. I will also have something to say about the wisdom and feasibility of current proposals to eliminate these defects.

The worst of these, if we may believe what we read in the newspapers and hear in Congress, is centered in the patched-up machinery through which we nominate and elect a President of the United States. Dissatisfaction with this machinery has been running strong ever since the election of 1800. It is a long time since anyone has commented on the electoral system with the smugness of Hamilton, who was frank to "affirm that if the manner of it be not perfect, it is at least excellent." Committee after committee, text after text, editorial after editorial have paraded before us the dangers and injustices of the system—especially those of the nominating conventions and the electoral college—and most Americans now assume that there is something wrong with it.

The case against the nominating convention is too familiar to bear repeating. In particular, I doubt that I need rehearse the cultural sins of which it is accused by sensitive observers. It should be enough to remind ourselves that this windy, vulgar circus is met to nominate a candidate for the most powerful office on earth, and to wonder if there could be any gathering of men that seems less in character with its high purpose, that seems more unhappily to express what Henry James called "the triumph of the superficial and the apotheosis of the raw." Yet the case against the convention falls finally to the ground, for the plain truth is that most criticisms of this noisy, plebeian, commercial institution are really criticisms of the noisy, plebeian, commercial civilization within which it operates. We see our follies as a people in the follies of the convention, and unless we reform ourselves, which I know we will not and suspect we dare not do, the convention will continue to disturb the reasonable, shock the fastidious, and fascinate all of us.

The technical charges against the nominating convention are that it is undemocratic, since it cuts the rank and file of the party out of the process of selecting a candidate; unreliable, since it ignores or distorts the real sentiment of the party in making the selection; and corrupt, since it puts a premium on the kind of horse trading in which men cannot expect to succeed unless they unlearn every rule of public and private morality. The convention, we are told, offers us a man we neither want nor deserve, and it offers him on a platter of corruption and cynicism. Those who make these charges usually go on to advocate some sort of nationwide presidential primary. The convention would become a pep rally to shout approval of the people's choice or, quite possibly, would be abolished altogether.

These charges, it seems to me, are a caricature of reality. The first and third might just as easily be leveled at Congress as at the nominating convention, while the second, which is most often and earnestly advanced, simply cannot stand up under the scrutiny of history. When in the twentieth century, except perhaps in the Republican convention of 1912, has a majority of the voters of either great party been handed a candidate it did not want? When, except in the nomination of Harding in 1920, did a convention pass over several first-rate men to choose an acknowledged second-rater? Quite to the contrary of accepted legend, the convention has done a remarkable job over the years in giving the voters of each party the man whom they, too, would have selected had they been faced with the necessity of making a responsible choice. The convention is anxious to satisfy, not frustrate, the hopes of the members of the party, and if the latter give an unmistakable sound, the former will echo it faithfully and gladly. If they speak in a babble of voices, if they cannot agree on a clear choice, the convention will choose their man for them, even if it take a hundred ballots, and the choice, moreover, will be made finally with near or complete unanimity. There is much to be said, of course, for the efforts of Senator Douglas and his friends to encourage the growth of presidential preference primaries. In nineteen states of the Union the voters of each party are now given some chance to elect or instruct their delegation to the convention. Yet it would be a mistake to make these useful exercises in public opinion much more uniform in pattern or binding in effect than they are at present. The convention works remarkably well; reformers should be careful not to upset the nice balance that history has struck between the hard responsibilities of the professionals at the convention and the vague wishes of the voters at home.

One can be more positive than this in defense of the convention, for it performs several tasks that no other institution or arrangement can perform as well if at all. Not only does it serve as the major unifying influence in political parties that are decentralized to the point of anarchy; it is, as Professor V. O. Key has written, "part and parcel of the magic by which men rule." And Americans, I again insist, are far from that enlightened condition in which political magic has lost its usefulness. The nominating convention fills a constitutional void; it unites and inspires each of the parties; it arouses interest in the grand plebiscite through which we choose our President. We will have to hear more convincing charges than have hitherto been pressed against the convention before we tamper with this venerable instrument of American democracy.

The case against the electoral system is more impressive, so impressive indeed that it led two-thirds of the Senate in 1950 to propose an amendment to the Constitution—the Lodge-Gossett (now Daniel) amendment—abolishing the electoral college, retaining the electoral vote, and dividing it within each state in exact proportion to the percentages of the popular vote cast for candidates for the Presidency. Not satisfied with this compromise between the old federal republic and the new continental democracy, Senator Humphrey advocates direct election of the President. Representative Coudert, on the other hand, favors a district system for registering the electoral vote. All these men unite in condemning the present system, especially those injustices and inconsistencies that arise from the "general ticket." Under this arrangement, which prevails throughout the Union, the total electoral vote in each state goes to the candidate with the highest popular vote. The chief criticisms of the resulting system seem to be these:

The electoral vote distorts, often radically, the real sentiment of the country.

Millions of votes for the Presidency go practically uncounted, and many Americans, at least in Vermont and Georgia, are doomed indefinitely to cast their presidential ballots in vain. As a result, many voters do not even bother to turn out.

It is entirely possible for us to elect, indeed we have several times elected, a "minority President"—a man who has not received even a plurality of the popular vote.

The parties are forced to concentrate much too heavily and corruptly on the large and unsure states, and minorities in these states swing political power out of all proportion to their size and importance.

The small states, even though overrepresented in the electoral count, are ignored as sources of presidential and even vice-presidential talent.

Harsh criticisms have also been aimed at other parts of the system. For example, some feel it potentially dangerous for the electors to retain, constitutionally and legally, their freedom of choice. Others argue that the House of Representatives, with each state delegation casting one vote, is about the last place in which a President should be chosen in the event that no one candidate secures an electoral majority. And we can all imagine the crisis that might develop if a President-elect were to die between the election in November and the casting of the electoral vote in December. There is no provision whatever, in Constitution or in law or in custom, for such a situation.

At least a dozen other arguments can be leveled against the dangers and inequities of the present system, and yet the system, having survived the challenge of 1950, bids well to endure in unreconstructed glory for years to come. The case against any constitutional amendment, which is largely political in inspiration, has been stated with refreshing frankness on the floors of both houses. The decisive obstruction to reform is apparently the general expectation that various minorities outside the South—in particular labor unions and ethnic groups—would lose much of their present hold over both parties, especially over the Democrats, if the presidential vote were to be divided in proportion to the popular vote of each state. This explains why the chief sentiment for rewriting the Twelfth Amendment is now centered in the conservative South, the chief sentiment for holding fast in the progressive North.

There is innate wisdom, if not always reasoned delicacy, in the stand of those who oppose drastic revision of the present system. One may take this stand for either or both of two solid reasons. The first is essentially conservative in mood and essence, for it is the argument of those who, recognizing that constitutional perfection is a cruel will-o'-the-wisp, would simply leave well enough alone. Such men, if I understand them rightly, are not unmindful of the defects of our electoral system. Yet they are sincerely convinced that a reformed system, from which all present dangers and injustices had been eliminated, would soon enough develop dangers and injustices of its own; and some of these might be far nastier than any we are asked to suffer at present.

They argue, further, that many of the dangers in the present system are hypothetical, many of the injustices not unjust at all. There is, for example, no indication that our political life has been hurt by distortions such as those registered in 1860 and 1936, and the American people should be given credit for ability to recognize an obvious distortion when they see one. There has been no convincing instance, certainly not in 1824 and 1876 and possibly not even in 1888, in which a candidate was cheated of the Presidency in spite of a clear plurality in the popular vote. An elector might exercise his alleged freedom of choice, as James Russell Lowell was implored unsuccessfully to do in 1876, but the chances that it could make any difference are one in ten thousand.

And so it goes with the whole attack on the present system: men who are understandably unsettled by the fantasy of our machinery for electing a President are determined to replace it with one that is simple and rational—no matter what new and unsuspected problems they may raise in the process. Such men, say defenders of the present system, are digging into the foundations of the state—always a dangerous thing to do, but especially in a time of watchful waiting.

The second argument is directed, at least in terms of current party politics, to liberal ends. The men who make it are frank to concede that the present electoral system is gerrymandered in favor of the urban vote, but this distortion, they assert, is a necessary counterbalance to the over-representation of rural interests in the House and Senate. The various proposals to eliminate the general ticket of electors in each state would upset the balance of representation in our total political system, and it would be even more difficult than at present for the forces of reform to come to grips with the problems of our industrial society. The Presidency, like Congress, would fall into the hands of the stand-patters rather than the progressives in each party. Indeed, the character of the Presidency as a great democratic office might well be jeopardized were its constituency thus altered.

Each of these arguments has much to be said for it, and for the present at least we should be content to rest upon

them and contemplate the electoral system with wry toler-
ance. There is no reason why we should not take immediate
steps to plug the gap between November 6 and December 17;
to provide that the House and Senate, with each member
casting one vote, be designated as the body for deciding in-
conclusive elections; and to encourage each state to institute
a presidential preference primary that gives clear counsel if
not a binding mandate to delegates to the convention. At the
same time, we might follow Senator Green's advice, lately
echoed by other members of Congress, and ask a joint congressional committee to inquire into such related questions
as the soundness of the present line of succession to the
Presidency and the possibility of devising some foolproof
means of determining presidential disability. The burden
of proof, however, should rest clearly upon those who think
they have found this "foolproof means."

There are several reasons, all of them convincing, why we
should hesitate a long time before replacing a humpty-
dumpty system that works with a neat one that may blow
up in our faces. Until we are sure that the Presidency itself
will not suffer from a radical change in the method of election, we had best stand fast on our traditional system.

A second defect that men find in the Presidency is the in-
tolerable burden laid upon him who holds it. I am not talking
here about the great functions of state he discharges in our
behalf, for I cannot imagine how a single one of these could
be transferred safely and effectively to some other officer in
the national government. It would be a constitutional disaster if the President were even to attempt to surrender his
final responsibility in the areas of war, peace, politics, opinion, ceremony, and management. I am talking, rather, of the
routine of these functions—of the mechanical tasks he is required to perform by law and custom; of the briefings, appointments, speeches, conferences, and appearances; of the
letters he must answer and signatures he must affix. Much
has been done in recent years to relieve him of his petty
burdens without relieving him of his great responsibilities,

and we can be grateful to the last three Presidents for having taken the lead in improving their own lot. Yet much, too, remains to be done. We should expect future Presidents, Congresses, and Executive Offices to co-operate in guarding the Presidency against the paralysis of detail. Considerable authority is already in the President's hands. For example, in 1950 Congress enacted a brief provision authorizing the President to delegate functions vested in him by statute, and we have the testimony of Sherman Adams that Mr. Eisenhower "has issued some sixty executive orders assigning literally hundreds of Presidential duties to the heads of Executive departments and other officials." We may be sure that every President from this time forward will press the search for functions to delegate to his chief lieutenants.

In seeking to lighten the President's burden, we would do well to recall the warning of Woodrow Wilson: "Men of ordinary physique and discretion cannot be Presidents and live, if the strain be not somehow relieved. We shall be obliged always to be picking our chief magistrates from among wise and prudent athletes—a small class." At the same time, we should also recall that a long list of routine tasks, each of which appears "nonessential" when viewed by itself, may well add up to an inspired performance of a great function of state. The President cannot be a successful Chief of State if he turns all the little ceremonies and visits over to the Vice-President. He cannot lead Congress if he is unwilling to spend hours listening to congressmen. And he cannot be a vigorous Commander in Chief unless he studies the defense budget item by item. For him as for all of us there is no final escape from hard and pedestrian labor. And as the gentlemen of Congress warned in the law of 1950 I have just mentioned: "Nothing contained herein shall relieve the President of his responsibility" for the acts of those "designated by him to perform [his] functions." As Mr. Truman would say, the President may pass the petty details but not the buck.

The Executive Office itself presents a number of problems, although it, too, is a huge improvement over the haphazard machinery on which our Presidents had to rely before 1939. For one thing, the President still lacks complete control over the organization of this machinery; he should be free to establish, regroup, or eliminate the components of the Executive Office on his own order and to experiment with the internal structure of each component. For another, there has never been a satisfactory arrangement within the Executive Office to assist him in handling his numerous duties as chief personnel officer of the national government. And for a third, he still lacks adequate assistance, in the form of a single staff agency or perhaps of several agencies, in co-ordinating the many elements in his total program.

The real problem of the Executive Office is potential rather than actual: the danger that the President might be buried under his own machinery. The institutionalization of the Presidency could be carried so far that the man who occupies it would become a prisoner in his own house, a victim of too much and too rigid organization. I doubt very much that such a situation could last for long if it did develop. Andrew Jackson proved once and for all the capacity of a determined President to burst the bonds of restrictive custom and legislation and to return to the plain words of Article II. Yet rather than make it necessary for another Jackson to blow across Washington like a "tropical tornado," we should be alert to steps that might weaken or smother the President's position of dominance over his own auxiliaries. Much depends, of course, on his intimate advisers. It is their unrelenting duty to protect the President against all but the most essential problems in their designated areas, to present these in such form that they can be readily mastered, and, above all, to preserve the President's freedom of choice among competing alternatives. Needless to say, the President himself must set the tone for the operations of the Executive Office. He must insist that he be spared routine but not thought and decision, for he is, after all, the responsible head of government. He must be careful not to rely too heavily on the briefings and opinions of his own staff, for he will soon find himself out of touch with harsh reality. Above all, he must leave channels open to the political and social pressures that excite imagination and breed sensitivity. Unfriendly visitors, hostile newspapers, and free-swinging press conferences are three such channels he must have the insight and bravery not to block off. The Presidency must never become so highly mechanized that the President himself is spared the suffering and glory of democratic leadership.

The Executive Office never will or should take on a permanent pattern of organization. Each President must feel free to tinker with it; no part of it, not even the Bureau of the Budget, should be considered too sacred to touch. The President, like the Red Queen, must run as fast as he can to stay in the same place. He must make a half-dozen adjustments in the course of his incumbency simply to keep pace with the rising tempo of his duties. The need in this vital area is for change and experiment, for an Executive Office that is not so much a perfect design as a plastic mosaic of formal and informal arrangements. There is, however, an outer limit beyond which it would be unwise to expand the Executive Office. It must be big enough to make it possible for the President to supervise the administration, but not so big that he has trouble supervising it.

The Cabinet has been a problem for at least a generation. Only tough custom and past glory have kept it from sliding noiselessly into oblivion. It is no longer a body upon which the President can rely for sage advice on great issues of state; it is not even, in its formal composition, a gathering of his most important and intimate associates. It is at best a relic of a simpler past when department heads were thought to be men of broad interests and held in their own hands the whole power of administration.

Mr. Eisenhower, to be sure, has done his best to restore the Cabinet to full duty. He has invited such key officials as the Director of the Budget and the Chairman of the Civil

Service Commission to attend regularly. He has gone ahead to institute what other Presidents only talked about vaguely: a formal Cabinet secretariat to organize its work, keep the necessary records, and follow through on decisions. In addition to setting up a sub-cabinet to support the Cabinet itself, he has continued the practice of authorizing Cabinet-level committees to deal with special problems, which in his incumbency have ranged all the way from the co-ordination of foreign aid activities to a drive on narcotics. He has even reminded us of the existence of the Cabinet by staging one of its sessions on television. At the same time, the President continues to use the National Security Council as a functional cabinet in matters of military and foreign policy, leaving the Cabinet to devote itself narrowly to domestic, administrative, and political affairs. A group that takes no real part in making and co-ordinating policy in the area of national survival can hardly be considered a great council of state.

It remains to be seen whether Mr. Eisenhower's efforts to revive the Cabinet will prove successful. He is bucking an ebb tide that has been running for a long time, and it is just possible that he and his successors could ride this tide to a happier solution. He needs conciliar advice, in national as in international affairs; he needs agencies to co-ordinate executive policy, in the government at large as in the White House. Yet it is clear that the Cabinet cannot serve these two high purposes as well as other groups and agencies that exist already or could be set up without too much difficulty. What would probably serve the President best is a series of functional cabinets and Cabinet-level committees, each with a secretariat of its own and each recognizing him or his deputy as chairman. The Cabinet itself, which has been around too long to be allowed to disappear entirely, might well be doubled in size and raised to the status of a privy council. It would meet only at moments of solemn decision; it would be a dignified holding company for the half-dozen sub-cabinets to which pertinent members of the parent body would belong. Though I tread here in fields of fancy, I think it altogether possible that the Cabinet's future lies in this direction.

Perhaps the softest spot of all in the general health of the Presidency lies in the gap between responsibility and authority, between promise and performance, in the area of public administration. The President, as I pointed out in Chapter 1, is held primarily responsible for the ethics, loyalty, efficiency, frugality, and responsiveness to the public's wishes of the two million and more Americans in the national administration. He is the Chief Executive, the general manager of the business of government, the one officer designated by the Constitution to "take care that the laws be faithfully executed." Yet his authority over the administration is in no way equal to his responsibility for its performance. Many executive functions are placed by statute beyond his reach in the independent commissions; many are carried on by bureaus and offices upon which time, tenure, and politics have bestowed an autonomy he challenges at his peril. Committees of Congress, themselves practically independent of their parent bodies, maintain more intimate relations with many agencies than those enjoyed by the President and his department heads. His own subordinates are often vested by statute with direct authority to conduct important programs; at the same time, they are granted appropriations in such detailed form that neither they nor the President can administer them with the necessary freedom of discretion. Almost everywhere the President turns to supervise and discipline, he is trapped in the toils of pluralism, tradition, politics, professionalism, and inertia.

Here, too, improvements have been wrought in recent years, although it is always a question whether these have kept pace with the careening growth of the administration. The most essential of these improvements, of course, was the incorporation of the Bureau of the Budget in the Executive Office, for without its help in both fiscal and administrative affairs the Presidency would long since have sunk without a trace. And here, too, much remains to be done, as the first Hoover Commission reminded the nation forcefully. Most of those who have lived with the problem and gone home to write about it agree that the President would benefit most as Chief Executive from these steps, no one of them easy to take:

The President should be granted full and permanent statutory power, subject to congressional disapproval within a specified time, to reorganize the internal structure of the executive branch; and then he should use this power to straighten out the lines of control throughout the administration.

Congress should help him to reduce the pockets of obstinate independence for whose existence there are not even convincing political reasons, and together they should work to cut down the number of officials whom the President is expected to supervise directly.

Congress should resist the urge to insert in the laws needlessly detailed instructions to those designated to execute them.

The President himself should experiment with groups and procedures designed to co-ordinate policy throughout the administration.

The whole system of personnel administration in the national government should be overhauled. On one hand, a reformed Civil Service Commission should be located within the Executive Office; on the other, the actual selection and management of personnel should be largely decentralized to department and commission heads.

We must not be misled by counsels of perfection in this confused area; we must not expect too much of the man who is supposed to supervise it. Inertia and tradition are found in all human organizations, and as often as not they serve some good purpose. There will always be conflict of purpose between the administrator with his professional knowledge and the politician with his constituency. In the very nature of things political and administrative, many tasks of government have to be performed with little or no opportunity for the application of over-all management. The "perfect pyramid" of administration is more a delusion than a panacea; rivalry and friction have virtues of their own. As long as power is both divided and shared by Congress and President, the former must be expected to take an active role in overseeing administration, and the role, as we know, can be played usefully as well as actively. The most essential point of all is to remember that the President has responsibilities that range far beyond his formless duty "to produce a good administration," and that many of these are impossible to delegate and disastrous to ignore. He has other and more important roles to play, and if he works too hard, if he succeeds too auspiciously, as Chief Executive, this is a certain sign that he is neglecting his high duties as Chief Diplomat or Commander in Chief.

It may well be time to readjust our thinking about the President's responsibility and authority as Chief Executive. If we cannot level the latter up, perhaps we should level the former down. We should not hold him to such strict account, as we still do in the country at large, for every blunder and fraud throughout the administration. He can never surrender constitutionally, nor should he surrender effectively, the final duty to oversee the execution of the laws. But we should ask no more of him than that he set a high personal example of integrity and industry, choose able men to administer the nation's business, delegate his administrative powers broadly and support his deputies faithfully, give a clear political lead that can be transmitted downward through his chief lieutenants, and act magisterially to punish glaring breaches of decorum and democracy. Perhaps we should be more tolerant of our Presidents.

Since the opening day of Washington's administration the President's relations with Congress have been a target of criticism; the target is still being shot at with enthusiasm and at least passing accuracy. Much of this criticism is irrelevant, since it ignores the blunt truth that we long ago made our irrevocable choice of co-ordinate rather than unified government. Much is softheaded, since it refuses to rise above the political and personal frictions that are the mark, but not the only mark, of such government. Yet much hits the target squarely, and I think we should take notice of two major areas in which the hope of improvement must never be abandoned.

In the first place, the President's leadership of Congress remains spotty and discontinuous. Although he is acknowledged widely to be the Leader of Legislation, his tools of persuasion, except his own machinery for drafting, clearing, and forwarding legislative proposals, are not one bit sharper than they were forty years ago. Here, too, as in the field of administration, there is a widening gap between what the people expect and what he can produce. He must have a program and push for its enactment, but he has no way to force a decision upon a reluctant Congress.

There have been a dozen or more proposals, some modest and others extravagant, to stabilize the President's leadership and increase his influence in Congress. Senator Kefauver has taken up Representative Pendleton's ancient plan for a question-and-answer period for department heads on the floor of either house. Professor Corwin predicts great gains for harmony if the President would choose part of his Cabinet from leading members of Congress. The La Follette-Monroney Committee of 1946 recommended a joint council of congressional leaders and Cabinet officers who would presumably work together in making and executing national policy. Some political scientists talk fondly of "responsible party government"; others put their trust in elaborate schemes for parallel organization of each major department or agency and its related committee in Congress. All these proposals are well-intentioned, and one, the establishment of an executive-legislative council by joint resolution, might be worth a try. Most, however, are not nearly so clever or feasible as they may seem at first glance, and several might have results far different from those predicted. In particular, it is not impossible that the President's leadership, which we have labored long to fix in custom, would suffer grave damage.

Is there nothing, then, that we can do to achieve a more stable relationship between the two great political branches? Nothing, I would answer, that ignores these facts, some of which I have already stated: First, superficial remedies will not cure, and may only quicken, the nervous tension between President and Congress that is endemic to our system. Second, stronger remedies, such as those proposed by Professor W. Y. Elliott and Thomas K. Finletter and David Lawrence, are just not called for in the present situation, nor would the patients submit to them in any situation. Third, we cannot have the best of both possible worlds, the rugged safeguards of our own system and the sweet harmonies of the British. To mix the metaphor hopelessly, there is no such thing as a happy mongrel that combines the good points of both parents. And finally, the affliction of dissension and irresponsibility arises from much deeper causes in our system than the arrangements of the Constitution. Those who insist that the affliction is a disease, and also think they can cure it, must go beyond government to reform politics and beyond politics to reform society—which is another way of saying that they should take the sage's advice to "relax and enjoy the inevitable."

In the last reckoning, we will continue to make progress toward firmer and friendlier executive-legislative relations by traveling the familiar path hacked out by the successful Presidents of this century. By following this path, even when it wandered through the swamps of petty politics, we have moved to a point at which co-operation under the President's guidance is far more certain than it was before 1900. Term by term, crisis by crisis, men in and out of Congress have been educated to accept the necessity of presidential leadership, and the Presidents have gone through a cumulative learning process of their own. This process of education in statesmanship must be carried on indefinitely, for in prescriptive growth, not in clever "gimmicks," lies our best hope for the co-operation we have a right to expect.

Most political observers are now more concerned with the other side of the two-way street between President and

Congress. While he is busy asserting leadership in making laws, Congress is busy asserting control over their execution, and there is evidence to support the charge that Congress has roamed farther out of bounds than the President in the past ten years. It is, to be sure, an axiom of co-ordinate government that the independent legislature must exercise oversight of the administration. Congress, too, must be concerned with ethics, loyalty, efficiency, frugality, and responsiveness in the public service; it must judge for itself whether the laws are being faithfully executed. No one can argue that it has any less constitutional right than the President to stake its claim to the disputed territory between them. But it does not have the right, probably not constitutionally and certainly not morally, to take over effective control of any part of the executive branch. It may inquire, expose, encourage, and warn, but it may not direct; and this—straight-out direction of various agencies and officers—is what Congress has been doing too much of in recent years. The result has been disorder, dissension, indecision, and disruption of morale at key points in the public service. Needless to say, Congress as a whole is guilty only of nonfeasance. It is the members of Congress, operating as committees, sub-committees, or lone wolves, who have poked their inquiring noses beyond the limits of political decorum and constitutional practice.

Concern over improper congressional meddling in the business of the executive reached a peak of indignation in the heady days when Senator McCarthy was asserting with implausible gall his right of espionage in the executive branch. It did seem for a while as if he and his friends might do permanent damage to those vague but visible lines drawn by custom between President and Congress. The decline of the Senator, matched and hastened by the rise of the President, has done much to restore the old condition of equilibrium in this delicate area. There are even those who feel that the lines were made more visible by Mr. Eisenhower's ordeal, or rather by the ordeal of those whom he seemed unwilling to protect; many members of Congress are now said to be more aware of the limits beyond which they cannot go in their search for misconduct in the administration. Surely we are all much clearer in our minds about the responsibility of the President and his chief lieutenants to keep Congress out of the executive sphere. It would be pleasant to think that each of the houses would have enough sense and bravery to hold its marauders in check, but while we await the Golden Age of congressional self-discipline, we must put our trust in the truth that power alone can check power. It is up to the President, exercising his rightful power, to hold the lines of constitutional sanity against those who would break through them in feckless quest of notoriety of sincere inquest of wrongdoing. He must defend his own authority while conceding that of Congress.

He has the best chance of doing this, it seems to me, by applying prudently this tested rule: the head of a department or agency, who has the power to give orders to his subordinates, must in turn stand ready to answer for the manner of their execution. The pertinent corollary is this: the head has the right and duty to interpose his authority—as best he can—between the investigator and the subordinate and give the necessary answers himself to congressional committees. In terms of recent experience, it was not a question of Senator McCarthy's right to ask "who promoted Major Peress," which we must concede with a grimace; it was a question of who should give the answer—the responsible head and his chief deputies, or a procession of bewildered and belabored subordinates. The responsible head, not a marauding Senator, must command the loyalty of the men for whose performance he is constitutionally and legally accountable. There are limits, of course, both political and practical, to the authority of a top administrator to control, defend, and speak for the public servants under his direction. Yet not until this wise old rule is established in our constitutional thinking will peace—as much peace as we can expect under our system—reign on this side of the street between President and Congress.

It may be thought irrelevant to call attention to the defects of Congress, but it is generally conceded that a strengthening of the national legislature in terms of its own internal structure would do much to improve working relations with the President. He has nothing to fear—to the contrary, he has much to gain—from the adoption of most proposals for reform that have been pressed on Congress by some of its best friends. Congress as a whole presents no improper threat to his legitimate control over the operations of the administration. Small groups and freewheeling individuals strike illicit bargains, plant co-operative friends, and ask indecent questions; small groups and freewheeling individuals hamstring the power of legislative decision and bring Congress into disrepute. Any step, therefore, that would lead to tighter organization—to a situation in which the houses could exercise some discipline over their outlaws and control over their obstructionists—would be a blessing alike to President and Congress. Any step toward efficiency—for example, a reduction in the number of committees—could not fail to give the President satisfaction. He has no stake in an inefficient and overburdened Congress. He has a sizable stake, as do all of us, in the reform of Congress.

There is one final defect in the relations of President and Congress of which we should take careful note, especially since its correction would strengthen the President's control over the administration as well as his influence in Congress. I refer to his lack of any power to veto separate items in the overstuffed appropriations bills presented for his approval. The President often feels compelled to sign bills that are full of dubious grants and subsidies rather than risk a breakdown in the work of whole departments. While it salves his conscience and cools his anger to announce publicly that he would veto these if he could, most congressmen have learned to pay no attention to his protests. The champions of the "item veto," who point out that thirty-nine governors have a power denied to the President, insist that nothing but great good would come from giving it to him— whether through a constitutional amendment or, failing that, a self-denying ordinance of Congress. On one hand, his leadership of Congress would be strengthened, for he would hold an efficient new weapon, one that works out in the open, for reminding congressmen that economy in the national interest is just as important as spending in the local interest. On the other, his work as Chief Executive would run more smoothly, since he would at last have full authority to match his responsibility for the executive budget. No agency of the government would be spending new money on a project of which he had the courage to disapprove sharply.

The loudest argument that has been raised against the item veto is that it might strengthen the President's hand just a little too much in his dealings with Congress. It would open the door to presidential pressure on individual congressmen, and thus to bargains of the hardest kind. There is much to be said for this argument, and we might well pause before amending the Constitution to grant this new power to the President. But there is no reason why Congress itself should not experiment with an occasional appropriations bill that authorizes the President to eliminate or reduce specific items subject to congressional reversal by concurrent resolution within a specified number of days. We have the assurance of several prominent constitutionalists that such a device would violate neither the letter nor the spirit of the Constitution. If Congress has given this power outright to the governors of several territories, it can certainly give it under wraps to the President of the United States. If we learn through these experiments that the power is one he ought to have, and is unlikely to abuse, we could then catch up with the Confederate States of America by writing it into the Constitution. We should hesitate much longer to grant him power to veto items in ordinary bills. Although the practice of attaching "riders" may often set our teeth on edge, Congress, too, needs weapons for the perpetual struggle, and we have no right to expect it to surrender this ancient blunderbuss.

Many Americans, not all of them Miniver Cheevys, would insist that I have thus far passed over with intent or in

ignorance the gravest defect in the Presidency: the high concentration of power that rests in the President's hands, the
startling expansion of this power over the past twenty-five
years, the frustrations that face Congress in the attempt to
regain its share and thereby to "restore the balance of the
Constitution." This was not my intent, nor am I ignorant
of this charge and the supporting evidence. No one who
pays even passing attention to American politics can fail to
know the full particulars of the case against the strong Presidency and the proposed steps to restore the old balance.
Senator Taft's challenge to Truman's initial action in Korea,
Representative Coudert's attempt to limit Eisenhower's
power to station troops in Europe by "rider," Senator
Bricker's campaign to reduce any President's power to negotiate treaties and agreements with other nations, Judge
Pine's restatement of the Whig or "errand-boy" theory of
the Presidency in the District Court decision in the Steel
Seizure case, Senator McCarthy's riotous assault on the first
principles of the Constitution—all these are straws, or whole
bales of hay, in a wind that beats relentlessly on the White
House. Challenges arise in every Congress to the scope if not
the existence of the President's power to adjust tariffs, issue
ordinances, make appointments, and influence the passage
of legislation. And in persuading the country to adopt the
Twenty-second Amendment, which forbids a third term, the
opponents of the strong Presidency have struck a mighty
blow for their cause.

Their cause, I am bound to say, is ill-considered and ill-
starred. It is ill-considered because any major reduction now
in the powers of the President would leave us naked to our
enemies, to the invisible forces of boom and bust at home
and to the visible forces of unrest and aggression abroad.
In a country over which industrialism has swept in great
waves, in a world where active diplomacy is the minimum
price of survival, it is not alone power but a vacuum of
power that men must fear. It is ill-starred because the Whigs,
who may win skirmishes and even an occasional battle, cannot win a war against American history. The strong Presi-

dency is the product of events that cannot be undone and of forces that continue to roll. We have made our decisions for the New Economy and the New Internationalism, and in making them we have made this kind of Presidency a requisite for the effective conduct of our constitutional system. No government can exercise the supervision that ours does over the economy at home or honor the bargains that ours has made abroad unless it has a strong, unified, energetic executive to lead it. I do not mean to say—I have not meant to say throughout this book—that "strength" in the Presidency is to be equated with "goodness" and "greatness." A strong President is a bad President, a curse upon the land, unless his means are constitutional and his ends democratic—unless he acts in ways that are fair, dignified, and familiar, and pursues policies to which a "persistent and undoubted" majority of the people has given support. We honor the great Presidents of the past, not for their strength, but for the fact that they used it to build a better America. And in honoring them we recognize that their kind of Presidency is one of our chief bulwarks against decline and chaos.

In point of fact, the struggle over the powers of the Presidency, fierce though it may seem, is only a secondary campaign in a political war over the future of America. Few men get heated up over the Presidency alone. Their arguments over its powers are really arguments over the American way of life and the direction in which it is moving. The strong Presidency is an instrument and symbol of 1956; the weak Presidency is an instrument and symbol of 1926. Those who truly yearn to "go home again," like John T. Flynn and Clarence Manion and the Daughters of the American Revolution, are right in thinking that a reduction in the powers of the Presidency would be an excellent first step to the rear—although it would be only a first step. It should be clearly understood that an attack on the Presidency like the Bricker Amendment is aimed beyond the Constitution at America's position in the world. The backers of this amendment may be greatly worried about the potential dangers of "presidential autocracy," but they are even more worried about the present consequences of the New Internationalism. Conversely, many voices that are raised for an even stronger Presidency are really raised for an even bigger government with even more control of society.

We should not look with equanimity on the Presidency and its huge arsenal of authority. We should be careful about giving the President additional powers, alert to abuses of those he already holds, cognizant that the present balance of the Constitution is not a cause for unlimited self-congratulation. But we can look on it with at least as much equanimity— each of us according to his own blend of blood, bile, phlegm, and melancholy—as we do upon the present state of the Union. For the strength of the Presidency is a measure of the strength of the America in which we now live. Those who accept this America and do not fear the one that is coming accept the strong Presidency soberly. Those who reject this America and are alarmed by the course we are taking reject the strong Presidency angrily.

As I look back through this book, I detect a deep note of satisfaction, although hardly of complacency, with the American Presidency as it stands today. A steady theme seems to have run all through this final review of its weaknesses and problems, a theme entitled—with apologies to the genius of Thurber—"Leave Your Presidency Alone!" This feeling of satisfaction springs, I am frank to admit, from a political outlook more concerned with the world as it is than as it is said to have been by reactionaries and is promised to be by radicals. Since this outlook is now shared by a staggering majority of Americans, I feel that I am expressing something more than a personal opinion. If we accept the facts of life in 1956, as we must, and if we shun the false counsels of perfection, as we do, then we are bound to conclude that we are richly blessed with a choice instrument of constitutional democracy. Judged in the light of memory and desire, the Presidency is in a state of sturdy health, and that is why we should not give way easily to despair over the defects men of too much zeal or too little courage claim to discover

in it. Some of these are not defects at all; some are chronic
in our system of government; some could be cured only by
opening the way to others far more malign.

This does not mean that we should stand pat with the
Presidency. Rather, we should confine ourselves to small re-
adjustments—I have noted a baker's dozen here that might
be worth a try—and leave the usual avenues open to prescriptive change. We should experiment in the states with presidential preference primaries but leave the electoral college
to pursue its illogical but hitherto effective way. We should
debate the question of stand-by controls in the event of war
with Bernard Baruch but take care that the inherent emergency power of the President—the power used by Lincoln
to blockade the South, by Wilson to arm the merchantmen,
and by Roosevelt to bring off the Destroyer Deal—be left
intact and untrammeled. We should experiment with a joint
executive-legislative council and the item veto but be on our
guard against the urge to alter radically the pattern of competitive coexistence between Congress and President. We
should give the President all the aides he can use but beware
the deceptively simple solution of a second Vice-President
for executive purposes. And we should tinker modestly with
the President's machinery but wake from the false dream of
perfect harmony in high places, especially in the highest place
of all. For if the Presidency could speak, it would say with
Whitman:

> Do I contradict myself?
> Very well then I contradict myself.
> (I am large, I contain multitudes.)

"Leave Your Presidency Alone"—that is the message of
this chapter, and I trust I have made clear in all these chapters why I transmit it so confidently. To put the final case for
the American Presidency as forcefully as possible, let me
point once again to its essential qualities:

It strikes a felicitous balance between power and limitations. In a world in which power is the price of freedom,
the Presidency, as Professor Merriam and his colleagues wrote
in 1937, "stands across the path of those who mistakenly as-

sert that democracy must fail because it can neither decide promptly nor act vigorously." In a world in which power has been abused on a tragic scale, it presents a heartening lesson in the uses of constitutionalism. To repeat the moral of Chapter 2, the power of the Presidency moves as a mighty host only *with* the grain of liberty and morality. The quest of constitutional government is for the right balance of authority and restraint, and Americans may take some pride in the balance they have built into the Presidency.

It provides a steady focus of leadership—of administration, Congress, and people. In a constitutional system compounded of diversity and antagonism, the Presidency looms up as the countervailing force of unity and harmony. In a society ridden by centrifugal forces, it is, as Sidney Hyman has written, the "common reference point for social effort." The relentless progress of this continental republic has made the Presidency our one truly national political institution. There are those who would reserve this role to Congress, but as the least aggressive of our Presidents, Calvin Coolidge, once testified, "It is because in their hours of timidity the Congress becomes subservient to the importunities of organized minorities that the President comes more and more to stand as the champion of the rights of the whole country." The more Congress becomes, in Burke's phrase, "a confused and scuffling bustle of local agency," the more the President must become a clear beacon of national purpose.

It is a priceless symbol of our continuity and destiny as a people. Few nations have solved so simply and yet grandly the problem of finding and maintaining an office of state that embodies their majesty and reflects their character. Only the Constitution overshadows the Presidency as an object of popular reverence, and the Constitution does not walk about smiling and shaking hands. "The simple fact is," a distinguished, disgruntled Briton wrote at the end of the "Royal Soap Opera" of 1955, "that the United States Presidency today is a far more dignified institution than the British monarchy." In all honesty and tact we must quickly demur, but we can be well satisfied with our "republican king."

It has been tested sternly in the crucible of time. Our obsession with youth leads us to forget too easily how long our chief instruments of government have been operating in unbroken career. The Presidency is now the most venerable excutive among all the large nations of the earth, and if one looks back beyond 1787 to "times of ancient glory and renown," he will find that the formula has worked before. "The truth is," Henry Jones Ford wrote with grace and insight,

> that in the presidential office, as it has been constituted since Jackson's time, American democracy has revived the oldest political institution of the race, the elective kingship. It is all there: the precognition of the notables and the tumultuous choice of the freemen, only conformed to modern conditions. That the people have been able . . . to make good a principle which no other people have been able to reconcile with the safety of the state, indicates the highest degree of constitutional morality yet attained by any race.

It is, finally, an office of freedom. The Presidency is a standing reproach to those petty doctrinaires who insist that executive power is inherently undemocratic; for, to the exact contrary, it has been more responsive to the needs and dreams of giant democracy than any other office or institution in the whole mosaic of American life. It is no less a reproach to those easy generalizers who think that Lord Acton had the very last word on the corrupting effects of power; for, again to the contrary, his doctrine finds small confirmation in the history of the Presidency. The vast power of this office has not been "poison," as Henry Adams wrote in scorn; rather, it has elevated often and corrupted never, chiefly because those who held it recognized the true source of the power and were ennobled by the knowledge. The American people, who are, after all, the best judges of the means by which their democracy is to be achieved, have made the Presidency their peculiar instrument. As they ready themselves for the pilgrimage ahead, they can take comfort and pride in the thought that it is also their peculiar treasure.

THE PRESIDENCY IN THE CONSTITUTION

☆

Those passages in the Constitution that touch directly upon the Presidency run as follows:

Article I

Section 3:

6. The Senate shall have the sole power to try all impeachments. When sitting for that purpose, they shall be on oath or affirmation. When the President of the United States is tried, the Chief Justice shall preside; and no person shall be convicted without the concurrence of two-thirds of the members present.

7. Judgment in cases of impeachment shall not extend further than to removal from office, and disqualification to hold and enjoy any office of honor, trust, or profit under the United States; but the party convicted shall, nevertheless, be liable and subject to indictment, trial, judgment, and punishment, according to law.

Section 7:

2. Every bill which shall have passed the House of Representatives and the Senate shall, before it become a law, be presented to the President of the United States; if he approve he shall sign it, but if not he shall return it, with his objections, to that house in which it shall have originated, who shall enter the objections at large on their journal and proceed to reconsider it. If after such reconsideration two-thirds of that house shall agree to pass the bill, it shall be sent, together with the objections, to

the other house, by which it shall likewise be reconsidered, and if approved by two-thirds of that house it shall become a law. But in all such cases the votes of both houses shall be determined by yeas and nays, and the names of the persons voting for and against the bill shall be entered on the journal of each house respectively. If any bill shall not be returned by the President within ten days (Sundays excepted) after it shall have been presented to him, the same shall be a law, in like manner as if he had signed it, unless the Congress by their adjournment prevent its return, in which case it shall not be a law.

3. Every order, resolution, or vote to which the concurrence of the Senate and House of Representatives may be necessary (except on a question of adjournment) shall be presented to the President of the United States; and before the same shall take effect, shall be approved by him, or being disapproved by him, shall be repassed by two-thirds of the Senate and House of Representatives, according to the rules and limitations prescribed in the case of a bill.

Article II
Section 1:

1. The executive power shall be vested in a President of the United States of America. He shall hold his office during the term of four years, and, together with the Vice-President, chosen for the same term, be elected as follows:

2. Each state shall appoint, in such manner as the legislature thereof may direct, a number of electors, equal to the whole number of Senators and Representatives to which the State may be entitled in the Congress; but no Senator or Representative, or person holding an office of trust or profit under the United States, shall be appointed an elector.

[3. The electors shall meet in their respective States and vote by ballot for two persons, of whom one at least shall not be an inhabitant of the same State with themselves. And they shall make a list of all the persons voted for, and of the number of votes for each; which list they shall sign and certify, and transmit sealed to the seat of the government of the United States, directed to the President of the Senate. The President of the Senate shall, in the presence of the Senate and House of Representatives, open all the certificates, and the votes shall then be counted. The person having the greatest number of votes shall be the President, if such a number be a majority of the whole number of electors appointed; and if there be more than one who have such majority, and have an equal number of votes, then the House of Representatives shall immediately choose by ballot one of them for President; and if no person have a majority, then from the five highest on the list the said House shall in like manner choose the President. But in choosing the President the votes shall be taken by States, the representation from each State having one vote; a quorum for this purpose shall consist of a member or members from two-thirds of the States, and a majority of all the States shall be necessary to a choice. In every case, after the choice of the President, the person having the greatest number of votes of the electors shall be the Vice-President. But if there should remain two or more who have equal votes, the Senate shall choose from them by ballot the Vice-President.]

4. The Congress may determine the time of choosing the electors and the day on which they shall give their votes, which day shall be the same throughout the United States.

5. No person except a natural born citizen, or a citizen of the United States at the time of the adoption of this Constitution, shall be eligible to the office of President; neither shall any person be eligible to that office who shall not have attained to the age of thirty-five years, and been fourteen years a resident within the United States.

6. In case of the removal of the President from office, or of his death, resignation, or inability to discharge the powers and duties of the said office, the same shall devolve on the Vice-President, and the Congress may by law provide for the case of removal, death, resignation, or inability, both of the President and Vice-President, declaring

what officer shall then act as President, and such officer shall act accordingly until the disability be removed or a President shall be elected.

7. The President shall, at stated times, receive for his services a compensation, which shall neither be increased nor diminished during the period for which he shall have been elected, and he shall not receive within that period any other emolument from the United States or any of them.

8. Before he enter on the execution of his office he shall take the following oath or affirmation:

"I do solemnly swear (or affirm) that I will faithfully execute the office of President of the United States, and will to the best of my ability preserve, protect, and defend the Constitution of the United States."

Section 2:

1. The President shall be Commander-in-Chief of the Army and Navy of the United States, and of the militia of the several States when called into the actual service of the United States; he may require the opinion, in writing, of the principal officer in each of the executive departments, upon any subject relating to the duties of their respective offices, and he shall have power to grant reprieves and pardons for offenses against the United States, except in cases of impeachment.

2. He shall have power, by and with the advice and consent of the Senate, to make treaties, provided two-thirds of the Senators present concur; and he shall nominate, and, by and with the advice and consent of the Senate, shall appoint ambassadors, other public ministers and consuls, judges of the Supreme Court, and all other officers of the United States, whose appointments are not herein otherwise provided for, and which shall be established by law; but the Congress may by law vest the appointment of such inferior officers, as they think proper, in the President alone, in the courts of law, or in the heads of departments.

3. The President shall have power to fill up all vacancies that may happen during the recess of the Senate, by grant-

ing commissions which shall expire at the end of their next session.

Section 3:

He shall from time to time give to the Congress information of the state of the Union, and recommend to their consideration such measures as he shall judge necessary and expedient; he may, on extraordinary occasions, convene both houses, or either of them, and in case of disagreement between them with respect to the time of adjournment, he may adjourn them to such time as he shall think proper; he shall receive ambassadors and other public ministers; he shall take care that the laws be faithfully executed, and shall commission all the officers of the United States.

Section 4:

The President, Vice-President, and all civil officers of the United States shall be removed from office on impeachment for and conviction of treason, bribery, or other high crimes and misdemeanors.

Amendment XII

The electors shall meet in their respective States and vote by ballot for President and Vice-President, one of whom, at least, shall not be an inhabitant of the same State with themselves; they shall name in their ballots the person voted for as President, and in distinct ballots the person voted for as Vice-President, and they shall make distinct lists of all persons voted for as President and of all persons voted for as Vice-President, and of the number of votes for each; which lists they shall sign and certify, and transmit sealed to the seat of the government of the United States, directed to the President of the Senate. The President of the Senate shall, in the presence of the Senate and House of Representatives, open all the certificates and the votes shall then be counted. The person having the greatest number of votes for President shall be the President, if such number be a majority of the whole number of electors appointed; and if no person have such

majority, then from the persons having the highest numbers not exceeding three on the list of those voted for
as President, the House of Representatives shall choose
immediately, by ballot, the President. But in choosing
the President the votes shall be taken by States, the representation from each State having one vote; a quorum
for this purpose shall consist of a member or members from
two-thirds of the States, and a majority of all the States
shall be necessary to a choice. And if the House of Representatives shall not choose a President whenever the right
of choice shall devolve upon them, before the fourth day
of March next following, then the Vice-President shall
act as President, as in the case of the death or other constitutional disability of the President.

The person having the greatest number of votes as Vice-
President shall be the Vice-President, if such number be a
majority of the whole number of electors appointed; and
if no person have a majority, then from the two highest
numbers on the list the Senate shall choose the Vice-President; a quorum for the purpose shall consist of two-thirds
of the whole number of Senators, and a majority of the
whole number shall be necessary to a choice. But no person constitutionally ineligible to the office of President
shall be eligible to that of Vice-President of the United
States.

Amendment XX

Section 1:

The terms of the President and Vice-President shall end
at noon on the 20th day of January, and the terms of
Senators and Representatives at noon on the 3d day of
January, of the years in which such terms would have ended
if this article had not been ratified; and the terms of their
successors shall then begin.

Section 2:

The Congress shall assemble at least once in every year,
and such meeting shall begin at noon on the 3d day of
January, unless they shall by law appoint a different day.

Section 3:

If, at the time fixed for the beginning of the term of the President, the President elect shall have died, the Vice-President elect shall become President. If a President shall not have been chosen before the time fixed for the beginning of his term, or if the President elect shall have failed to qualify, then the Vice-President elect shall act as President until a President shall have qualified; and the Congress may by law provide for the case wherein neither a President elect nor a Vice-President elect shall have qualified, declaring who shall then act as President, or the manner in which one who is to act shall be selected, and such person shall act accordingly until a President or Vice-President shall have qualified.

Section 4:

The Congress may by law provide for the case of the death of any of the persons from whom the House of Representatives may choose a President whenever the right of choice shall have devolved upon them, and for the case of the death of any of the persons from whom the Senate may choose a Vice-President whenever the right of choice shall have devolved upon them.

Amendment XXII

No person shall be elected to the office of the President more than twice, and no person who has held the office of President, or acted as President, for more than two years of a term to which some other person was elected President shall be elected to the office of the President more than once. But this Article shall not apply to any person holding the office of President when this Article was proposed by the Congress, and shall not prevent any person who may be holding the office of President, or acting as President, during the term within which this Article becomes operative from holding the office of President or acting as President during the remainder of such term.

Appendix II

THE PRESIDENTS OF
THE UNITED STATES

	Date of Inauguration	Age at Inauguration	State of Residence	Politics	Date of Death
George Washington	1789	57	Va.	Fed.	1799
John Adams	1797	61	Mass.	Fed.	1826
Thomas Jefferson	1801	57	Va.	Dem.-Rep.	1826
James Madison	1809	57	Va.	Dem.-Rep.	1836
James Monroe	1817	58	Va.	Dem.-Rep.	1831
John Q. Adams	1825	57	Mass.	Dem.-Rep.	1848
Andrew Jackson	1829	61	Tenn.	Dem.	1845
Martin Van Buren	1837	54	N. Y.	Dem.	1862
William H. Harrison	1841	68	Ohio	Whig	1841
John Tyler	1841	51	Va.	Whig	1862
James K. Polk	1845	49	Tenn.	Dem.	1849
Zachary Taylor	1849	64	La.	Whig	1850
Millard Fillmore	1850	50	N. Y.	Whig	1874
Franklin Pierce	1853	48	N. H.	Dem.	1869
James Buchanan	1857	65	Pa.	Dem.	1868
Abraham Lincoln	1861	52	Ill.	Rep.	1865
Andrew Johnson	1865	56	Tenn.	Dem. (Union)	1875
Ulysses S. Grant	1869	46	Ill.	Rep.	1885
Rutherford B. Hayes	1877	54	Ohio	Rep.	1893
James A. Garfield	1881	49	Ohio	Rep.	1881
Chester A. Arthur	1881	50	N. Y.	Rep.	1886
Grover Cleveland	1885	47	N. Y.	Dem.	1908
Benjamin Harrison	1889	55	Ohio	Rep.	1901
Grover Cleveland	1893	55	N. Y.	Dem.	1908
William McKinley	1897	54	Ohio	Rep.	1901
Theodore Roosevelt	1901	42	N. Y.	Rep.	1919
William H. Taft	1909	51	Ohio	Rep.	1930
Woodrow Wilson	1913	56	N. J.	Dem.	1924
Warren G. Harding	1921	55	Ohio	Rep.	1923
Calvin Coolidge	1923	51	Mass.	Rep.	1933
Herbert Hoover	1929	54	Cal.	Rep.	—
Franklin D. Roosevelt	1933	51	N. Y.	Dem.	1945
Harry S. Truman	1945	60	Mo.	Dem.	—
Dwight D. Eisenhower	1953	62	N. Y.	Rep.	—
John F. Kennedy				Dem.	
Lyndon B. Johnson				Dem.	
Richard M. Nixon				Rep.	

INDEX